SOUTH WEST & SOUTH WALES
INDEPENDENT
GIN
& ARTISAN
SPIRITS
guide

EDITION
2

Copyright © Salt Media Ltd

Published by Salt Media Ltd 2019

01271 859299

Email: ideas@saltmedia.co.uk

www.saltmedia.co.uk

Salt Media *Independent Gin & Artisan Spirits Guide* team:
Susy Atkins, Richard Bailey, Katie Comer, Nick Cooper,
Sophie Ellis, Kathryn Lewis, Abi Manning,
Tamsin Powell, Calandra Redfearn, Jo Rees, Rosanna Rothery,
Amy Sargeant, Christopher Sheppard, Yohann Thuillier,
Josephine Walbank, Linda Weller and Selena Young.

Design and illustration: Salt Media

A big thank you to headline sponsor Luscombe Drinks **and
sponsors** Dartington Crystal, Salcombe Distilling Co. and
The Wrecking Coast Distillery.

Distilleries, bars, retailers and gin schools are invited to be included
in the guide based on meeting strict and very high criteria, which,
in the case of distilleries includes distilling the drinks themselves in
small batches, being independently owned and run and providing
a high quality spirits experience. Bars and retailers are required to
stock at least five of the spirits eligible for entry in the guide and in
the case of bars, provide a specific serve for each of these spirits.

www.indygin.guide

@indyginguide

@indyginguide

Independent Gin Guide

Photo: Matt Austin Images

42
Doctor Ink's Curiosities, Exeter

CONTENTS

WELCOME

L ast year we published the first *South West Independent Gin Guide*, a book revealing the region's incredible true-craft gin scene.

Twelve months on, we're witnessing a similar resurgence in a wider range of spirits, just as meticulously crafted and boasting equally impeccable provenance. So, in this second edition, we've opened the drinks cabinet to other exquisite sips and cast the net wider to include South Wales.

There are some devastatingly good drinks being devised right now and it feels a little like that creative and entrepreneurial moment in the early noughties when the UK food revolution really started taking off.

We're on another leg of that same journey, I believe, and it looks like it's leading to increasingly interesting, authentic and carefully crafted spirits - and unique ways to experience them.

Jo Rees
Editor

🐦 @indyginguide
📷 @indyginguide
f Independent Gin Guide

100% (FUTURE) PROOF

Drinks expert **Susy Atkins** distils some of the new trends in the ever-changing world of craft spirits

At least once a week I used to get asked when the gin bubble would burst. Now it's clear that premium gin is here to stay.

The days of one option on the optic, tired tonic and limp lemon are over. I'm far more likely to be debating the next exciting chapter in the ever-evolving gin-naissance and world of fine spirits than any imminent demise.

So where next? What are the trends now and how will they influence the way we enjoy spirits in the next year or two?

Let's stick with gin for the moment. April Marks of Regency Wines in Exeter stocks a huge range of gin

and, when quizzed about the future, points immediately to the rise of high quality flavoured gins in the past few months.

'*There are so many now that it has become a crowded market*,' she says. '*Unbalanced flavours will mask a gin, but some distilleries are really getting it right.*'

She singles out Salcombe Gin's new 'Rosé Sainte Marie' with its delicate pink colour and dry flavour as '*absolutely spot on*'. Sweet and sticky alcopops these are most certainly not.

Joel Harrison and Neil Ridley, authors of the newly published *World Atlas of Gin* agree.

'FRUIT GINS AND GIN LIQUEURS ARE RIDING HIGH'

'Flavoured gins continue to gather pace,' says Joel. *'It's a fantastic example of where the consumer is leading the way.'*

The region's top gin palaces are finding favour with flavoured gins too. Dolly Makin of Dolly's Tea Room in Falmouth reports that fruit gins and gin liqueurs are riding high. Their bright juicy flavours often suit those who don't like plain tonic, as these drinks are also great topped up with the likes of ginger ale, lemon tonic and Prosecco. In this guide you'll find some wonderful flavoured gins - and we predict they'll prove even more popular over the next year.

Cocktails are as popular as ever but the highly theatrical, complex style of presentation, while still most definitely hip, is being rivalled by a new stripped-back, dialled-down look. Patrick Fogarty of the award winning Doctor Ink's Curiosities bar on Exeter's quayside (and new Teignmouth seafront bar Halulu) is the king of the stylised Victorian cocktail but he has spotted a trend for minimalist concoctions lately.

'These are purist drinks, just three or four ingredients served in an unremarkable plain glass, with just one big lump of ice and no garnish at all.' He describes the look as Scandi-influenced and contemporary.

'THERE'S NOW A REAL BUZZ AROUND RUM'

So which spirits, apart from gin, are being shaken up into those cocktails? One word: rum. As Patrick says: *'There's now a real buzz around rum. People are asking for it by specific brand and are enjoying spiced and flavoured rums massively.'*

Rum drinking – either sipping the spirit on the rocks, in cocktails or as a rum and tonic (every bit as good as a great G&T) – is en vogue this year. And with rum's sweet and warming qualities, it'll doubtless remain popular through the winter months.

Two other trends are particularly welcome. The first is the rise in sustainable and environmentally friendly practices in both distilleries and bars. We've referred in this guide to several spirits companies taking sustainability seriously – see Ramsbury Gin's single estate methods.

In bars, keeping waste to a minimum is becoming key and refilled bottles from five-litre reusable pouches are now a thing.

At home, I'm sure many of us cannot bear to part with the most

'THERE ARE A LOT OF GORGEOUS EX-GIN-BOTTLE VASES AROUND ...'

beautiful empty spirits bottles. There are a lot of gorgeous ex-gin-bottle vases around ...

Inextricably linked to eco developments is the trend for buying local. Bartenders report that provenance is more important than ever, with many spirits drinkers specifically requesting local brands. Dolly Makin reports that special local gin-menus which group together the regional brands are now popular, and I reckon we'll see more of these.

'Hyper-local spirits are huge,' agrees Joel Harrison of the *World Atlas of Gin.* *'This means, as with real ales, you can drink something conceived and distilled locally using botanicals which reflect the local terroir. It may also mean you can visit the producer to see the process and meet the people behind the stills.'*

It's this sense of local provenance that's inspired the guide and is well worth raising a glass to.

EXCEPTIONALLY INDEPENDENT

Exceptional gins deserve exceptional mixers.
The range of mixers from Luscombe Drinks in Devon
goes way beyond the usual tonic – it opens up a world
of creative possibilities.

G&T lover? You'll be spoilt for choice as the Luscombe
range also includes cucumber, grapefruit, elderflower,
Devon and Devon light tonic varieties to complement
even the most unusual botanicals.

HEADLINE
SPONSOR OF

SOUTH WEST & SOUTH WALES
INDEPENDENT
GIN
& ARTISAN
SPIRITS
guide
EDITION
2

LUSCOMBE.CO.UK

The Xtraction factor

Drinks maestro **Yohann Thuillier** reveals how extracting flavours using a cream whipper is expanding creative horizons on the bar

Just imagine the fun you could have infusing spirits with all your favourite flavours. Parma Violets vodka? Vanilla sponge sherry? The implication are intoxicating.

It's no surprise, then, that drinks pros like Yohann (who oversees the bar experience at The Greenbank Hotel in Falmouth and The Alverton in Truro) are excited by the opportunities that a cream whipper and a special infusion technique present.

'We love playing with flavours and creating new ways to surprise the palate by putting together drinks with flavours and aromas you can't find anywhere else,' says Yohann. *'We do it using Dave Arnold's relatively quick and easy Rapid Infusion Technique.'*

Arnold is the food science writer, educator and innovator who runs the high-tech cocktail bar Booker & Dax in New York's East Village.

When cream whipper company ISI asked him to play around with their whippers to see if he could find some new applications for the equipment, he was never going to come up with just any old thing.

'Parma Violets vodka or vanilla sponge sherry?'

'*What he created,*' says Yohann, '*was a technique that allows the transfer of flavours from a solid to a liquid in a very short amount of time.*

'*Before that, the only way to infuse a liquid* [with other flavours] *was slow, involving steeping the solids in the liquid for days, weeks or months, or it was expensive due to the use of equipment like a Rotavap* [a rotary evaporator as used in chemistry labs].

Orange and rosemary infused gin

Makes 1 bottle

You will need

Cream whipper
Jug
Fine mesh strainer or muslin cloth
Nitrous oxide cartridges 2

Oranges 3 large, zested (avoid the pith as it will make the gin bitter)
Fresh rosemary 50g
Dry gin 70cl

Method

Place the orange zest and rosemary into the tin of the whipper, then pour in the gin.

Screw the lid on and add the first cartridge of nitrous oxide.

Shake well and wait for 20 minutes. Remove the first cartridge and add the second one (keeping the lid on). Let it rest for another 20 minutes.

Remove the second cartridge and vent the whipper by depressing the lever. Cover the nozzle with the jug as it may spit some liquid out.

Remove the lid. You should see the liquid bubbling, which means the extraction is taking place.

Once the liquid stops bubbling, strain it into the jug. For an even clearer result, strain through a muslin cloth.

Allow the infusion to rest for 10 minutes, then rebottle or use straight away.

'Another issue with steeping is that you are likely to also extract compounds which are not wanted and could potentially ruin a whole batch by adding too much bitterness.'

When Arnold wrote about his discoveries in his book *Liquid Intelligence: The Art and Science of the Perfect Cocktail*, the drinks industry jumped on the method and it soon become a staple of very good cocktail bars.

'The method is quick, cheap and reliable,' says Yohann. *'It relies on just a cream whipper and nitrous oxide (N_2O), a colourless water/ethanol/fat-soluble, slightly sweet-tasting gas which comes in small cartridges.*

'The advantage of this technique is that any liquid can potentially be infused with any solid as long as the solid is porous; in fact the more porous it is, the easier it is to extract flavours.

'To give it a go, all you need is a cream whipper (an ISI one preferably) and some N_2O cartridges, which are both readily available on the high street or online,' says Yohann.

Feeling creatively inspired? Give Yohann's recipe for orange and rosemary infused gin a whirl and then turn it into a Provençal Collins.

Provençal Collins

Orange and rosemary infused gin 50ml
Sugar syrup 25ml
Fresh lime juice 20ml
Soda

Build over ice in a highball glass and garnish with a sprig of rosemary and orange zest.

HOW TO
USE THE GUIDE

We've split the information into sections to make the guide as clear as a crisp gin and tonic

SPIRITS OF DISTINCTION
Artisan spirits crafted by independent alchemists.

EXCEPTIONALLY AGREEABLE HAUNTS
Beautiful bars and lounges for libation.

PURVEYORS OF IMPECCABLE SPIRITS
Where to stock your drinks cabinet with unusual and specialist finds.

BACK TO SCHOOL
Develop your distilling skills.

MAPS AND NUMBERS
Every spirit, bar, retailer and school has a number so you can find them on the map on page 24 or in the index at the back of the book.

Don't forget to let us know how your adventures unfold. Share your pictures and finds with us at

🐦 @indyginguide
📷 @indyginguide
f Independent Gin Guide

WWW.INDYGIN.GUIDE

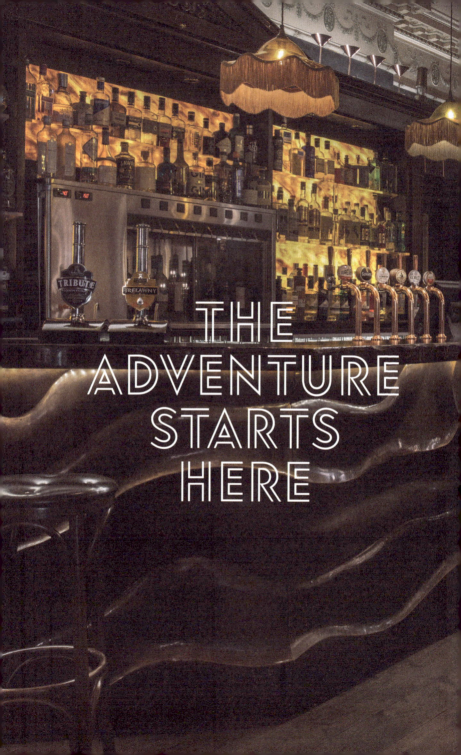

57
Penventon Park Hotel

SPIRIT CONNOISSEURS' MAP

Find establishments in the guide by the number at the top of each page

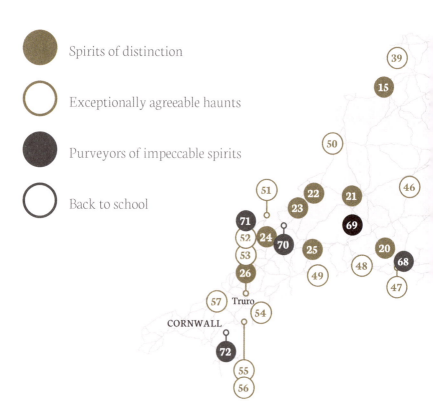

Spirits of distinction

Exceptionally agreeable haunts

Purveyors of impeccable spirits

Back to school

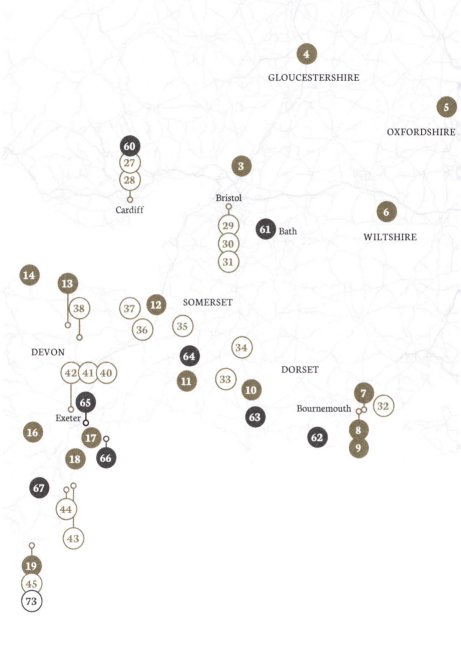

GLOUCESTERSHIRE

OXFORDSHIRE

Cardiff

Bristol

Bath

WILTSHIRE

SOMERSET

DEVON

DORSET

Bournemouth

Exeter

Locations are approximate

SPIRITS OF DISTINCTION

Artisan sips crafted by independent alchemists

1 CINNAMON GROVE GIN

The story of Cinnamon Grove Gin began with water taken from a 300-year-old well on the family farm near Haverfordwest in Pembrokeshire.

Its pure quality inspired an experiment in gin making, which was so successful that it eventually led to the creation of the region's first gin distillery.

It's the use of the water in the production of the spirit that's believed to be the secret behind this distinctively smooth gin.

The perfectly balanced spirit contains 11 carefully selected botanicals and is handcrafted in small batches at Cinnamon Grove Farm in a copper still named Ruby.

DISTILLERY
Cinnamon Grove

ESTABLISHED
2018

DRINK LAUNCHED
2018

LITRES PER YEAR
2,000

SISTER SPIRITS
Cinnamon Grove

Premium Pink Gin

PERFECT POURS

GIN AND TONIC

Serve with a light premium tonic and garnish with red grapefruit and lime.

GINGER GROVE

Pour a measure into a large copa glass filled with ice, then top up with light ginger ale. Garnish with lemon and lime for extra zing.

www.cinnamongrovegin.co.uk   07496 906309

Cinnamon Grove Farm, Old Hakin Road, Haverfordwest, Pembrokeshire, SA61 1XG

TASTING NOTES

-

A rich and generously flavoured gin with
a juniper scent, fresh streak of citrus and
warm earthy and spicy notes. Balanced and
soft on the finish.

-

ABV 42.9%

2 JIN TALOG SINGLE BOTANICAL ORGANIC GIN

If you favour a traditional gin, then Jin Talog is one for you as the distinctive and uncompromising spirit uses only one botanical: juniper.

Its natural oils are gently coaxed out using a secret method to guarantee peak flavour of this key and organic ingredient.

'Jin' is Welsh for gin, and the name makes sense when you discover that the spirit is made in rural Carmarthenshire on a farm in Talog – the only dedicated gin distillery in the county. It's produced in nano-batches of just 30 bottles at a time in a former cowshed using spring water from the farm.

Try sipping Jin Talog with Scandinavian food. It's also a delicious ingredient when used to cure salmon, as well as in gin jellies and pannacotta.

DISTILLERY
Jin Talog

ESTABLISHED
2018

DRINK LAUNCHED
2018

LITRES PER YEAR
2,800

SISTER SPIRITS
Jin Talog Limited Edition Twin Botanical Organic Gins

DISTILLERY TOURS
Available by appointment

SOLD ON SITE

PERFECT POURS

GIN AND TONIC

Enjoy neat over ice or in a classic G&T: serve with plenty of ice in a tumbler, using the ratio of 1:2 gin to tonic. Avoid citrus which may distract from the juniper.

COCTEL Y CLAWDD (HEDGEROW COCKTAIL)

Jin Talog 25ml
Cointreau 10ml
Chambord Raspberry Liqueur 10ml
Fever-Tree Elderflower Tonic 125ml
Raspberry 1

Mix the gin and liqueurs and serve over ice. Top up with tonic and garnish with a raspberry.

www.jintalog.wales   01994 284011
Y Ddistyllfa, Rhyd Y Garreg Ddu, Talog, Carmarthenshire, SA33 6NN

TASTING NOTES

Jin Talog's aromas and flavour showcase fine juniper with clean notes of pine and leafy, earthy forest floor, with a savoury edge. Strong and bold, this is a gin that will easily stand out over tonic.

-

ABV 42%

3 6 O'CLOCK GIN

6 O'clock Gin, in its stunning Bristol blue glass bottle, is named after a family tradition of indulging in a G&T at exactly six o'clock each evening.

Head distiller Edward founded Bramley & Gage in 1988, originally making fruit liqueurs in south Devon. He developed an old family gin recipe in order to create Bramley & Gage's first sloe gin, and this London dry was later perfected by his children Michael and Felicity (who now run the business).

6 O'clock is traditional in style with juniper aromas sitting alongside other carefully selected botanicals including elderflower, winter savory and orange peel.

DISTILLERY
6 O'clock Gin

ESTABLISHED
1988

DRINK LAUNCHED
2010

LITRES PER YEAR
70,000

SISTER SPIRITS
Brunel Edition

Damson Gin

DISTILLERY TOURS
Available

PERFECT POURS

GIN AND TONIC

Use plenty of ice, good tonic and a lemon twist for a refreshing, classic G&T. As the clock strikes 6pm, naturally ...

FLORODORA

6 O'clock Gin 50ml
Raspberry liqueur 20ml
Lime juice 15ml
Ginger ale to top up
Lime slice to garnish
Fresh raspberries to garnish

Build the drink in a highball glass over plenty of ice. Add the gin, raspberry liqueur and lime juice and stir, then top up with ginger ale. Garnish with the lime and raspberries.

www.6oclockgin.com 01454 418046

Ashville Park, Short Way, Thornbury, Bristol, BS35 3UU

TASTING NOTES

-

A gin of true elegance: soft, crisp and clean, leading with juniper before revealing further notes of elderflower and subtle spice with a citrus twist on the finish.

-

ABV 43%

4 TWISTING SPIRITS
DOUGLAS-FIR DISTILLED GIN

Mary and Richard Bateman founded Twisting Spirits with the clear aim of creating distinctive and unusual gins with massive bursts of flavour.

They use a dual process: a fine gin is made in traditional copper stills, while Douglas-Fir tree needles are cold distilled under vacuum in a rotary evaporator to preserve their more delicate characteristics.

These needles are foraged every autumn from selected trees. Together with bright juniper and other botanicals including cassia bark, orris root and cubeb pepper, they deliver a highly original gin.

DISTILLERY
Twisting Spirits

ESTABLISHED
2017

DRINK LAUNCHED
2017

LITRES PER YEAR
5000

SISTER SPIRITS
Kaffir Lime & Lemongrass Distilled Gin

Earl Grey Tea Distilled Gin

PERFECT POURS

GIN AND TONIC

Douglas-Fir Gin 50ml
Premium unflavoured tonic 100ml
Red grapefruit slice to garnish

Serve in a highball glass with plenty of ice.

TWISTED PALOMA

Douglas-Fir Gin 50ml
Fresh lime juice 15ml
Fresh red grapefruit juice 50ml
Soda water
Grapefruit twist to garnish

Add the gin and juices to a collins glass filled with ice. Top with soda water to taste and garnish with the grapefruit twist.

www.twistingspirits.co.uk   07709 359203

Oldbury Buildings, Northway Lane, Tewkesbury, Gloucestershire, GL20 8JG

TASTING NOTES

-

Whistle-clean herbaceous and
fresh pine qualities pervade the
aroma and flavour. Look out for
nuances of crisp citrus, cut grass
and white pepper. A tongue-
tingling, richly textured gin.

-

ABV 41.5%

5 KEEPR'S LONDON DRY GIN WITH BRITISH HONEY

The delicate sweetness of pure, unadulterated Cotswolds honey gives a delightful twist to this otherwise classic London dry gin.

Busy workers at The British Honey Company make the gin in small batches of just 300-500 bottles, and each is traceable to the very hive in west Oxfordshire where the honey was sourced.

Master distiller James Baggot draws upon more than a decade of experience in crafting award winning spirits in the Keepr's range, and has created a wonderful infusion of a local ingredient with a premium spirit.

DISTILLERY
The British Honey Company

ESTABLISHED
2014

DRINK LAUNCHED
2017

LITRES PER YEAR
50,000

SISTER SPIRITS
British Raspberry & Honey Gin

1606 London Dry Gin

PERFECT POURS

GIN AND TONIC

Keepr's Honey Gin 50ml
Tonic of your choice
Fresh lime a wedge
Rosemary a sprig

Fill a glass with ice and pour in the gin. Top up with tonic to taste and garnish with the lime and rosemary.

BEE'S KNEES

Keepr's Honey Gin 50ml
Lemon juice 20ml
Orange juice 20ml
Bitters a dash
Fresh citrus zest to garnish
Keepr's British Honey to garnish

Shake the liquids together in a cocktail shaker with ice, then single strain into a coupé glass, allowing the foam to settle. Garnish with zest and a drizzle of honey.

www.britishhoney.com   01993 880597
PO BOX 398, Kidlington, Oxfordshire, OX5 9EW

TASTING NOTES

-

The irresistible flavour of pure,
natural honey pervades this spirit.
It's carefully balanced and not overly
sweet, with a soft rounded finish: a
perfect pairing for blue cheese.

-

ABV 40%

RAMSBURY GIN

Ramsbury, near Marlborough, is one of only a handful of single estate distilleries.
Will Thompson and co create spirits from scratch using Estate-grown horatio wheat and water from their own chalk-filtered water source, and heat the stills with sustainably sourced biomass from the Estate's forest.

The team started as farmers and are proud to have remained so, despite founding a brewery in 2004, which was followed by the distillery in 2016.

Fresh quince is a key botanical in Ramsbury Gin and is accompanied by eight others, including dried citrus peel, cinnamon and liquorice. It's perfect served on its own over ice.

DISTILLERY
Ramsbury Distillery

ESTABLISHED
2016

DRINK LAUNCHED
2017

SISTER SPIRITS
Ramsbury Single Estate Vodka

DISTILLERY TOURS
Available

SOLD ON SITE

PERFECT POURS

GIN AND TONIC

Ramsbury Gin makes a delicious G&T garnished with fresh green apple and lime slices.

THE BELL

Ramsbury Gin 40ml
Apricot liqueur 25ml
Supasawa mixer a dash
Soda water
Black olive 1
Rosemary a sprig

Mix the gin, liqueur and Supasawa over ice, then strain into a glass and top up with soda. Garnish with the black olive and rosemary.

www.ramsbury.com   01672 541407
Stockclose Farm, Aldbourne, Wiltshire, SN8 2NN

TASTING NOTES

-

Clean and fresh-tasting with
a cereal element to the aroma
and a distinctive juicy flavour
of quince (similar to pears and
apples combined). The texture is
smooth, almost creamy.

-

ABV 40%

7 POTHECARY GIN

Pothecary's bold botanicals include lavender, black mulberries, lemon and linden flowers alongside Serbian juniper. Each is distilled separately before being blended together and cut with New Forest spring water.

The result is a gin of superb clarity and bright flavours which has also been certified organic by the Soil Association.

Enjoy this deeply aromatic and smooth gin as a true sipping spirit or pair it with simple raw fish dishes such as sashimi and ceviche. It can even be used as a cure for salmon or mackerel.

DISTILLERY
Soapbox Spirits

ESTABLISHED
2016

DRINK LAUNCHED
2016

LITRES PER YEAR
5,000 - 8,000

SISTER SPIRITS
Sicilian Blend
Trinity Blend

DISTILLERY TOURS
Available

SOLD ON SITE

PERFECT POURS

SIPPING STYLE

Pour 50ml Pothecary Gin over two large blocks of ice in a rocks tumbler.

Garnish with two thin strips of lemon or orange peel, twisted to release the oils.

ROYAL FIZZ

Pothecary Gin 25ml
Earl grey tea syrup or elderflower syrup 5-10ml
English sparkling wine to top up
Lemon zest to garnish

Pour the gin and syrup into a tall flute glass, then top up with the wine. Garnish with a twist of lemon zest.

www.pothecarygin.co.uk   07534 804917
91 Stour Road, Christchurch, Dorset, BH23 1JN

TASTING NOTES

-

The fresh and summery aroma
of lavender is followed by juicy,
fruity citrus and mulberry with
plenty of juniper. The gin ends
richly and smoothly with a lightly
oily, honeyed hint.

-

ABV 44.8%

8 CONKER SPIRIT RNLI NAVY STRENGTH GIN

Conker Spirit was founded by Rupert Holloway in 2014 with the launch of its award winning, small-batch Dorset Dry Gin.

Then, in 2018, the Bournemouth distillery introduced its RNLI Navy Strength Gin to the world.

The hearty and robust gin is distilled in honour of the Royal National Lifeboat Institution, and Conker supports the RNLI's mission of saving lives at sea by giving £5 to the charity for every bottle sold.

A classically styled gin, this is strong but balanced, with bold juniper paired with seville orange and herbaceous notes from marsh samphire and elderberries.

DISTILLERY
Conker Spirit

ESTABLISHED
2014

DRINK LAUNCHED
2018

LITRES PER YEAR
40,000

SISTER SPIRITS
Dorset Dry Gin

DISTILLERY TOURS
Available

SOLD ON SITE

PERFECT POURS

RNLI NAVY STRENGTH G&T

The forthright juniper and seville orange in this gin means a 25ml serving is perfect.

Top it up with classic indian tonic water and garnish with a thin strip of orange peel.

GIN MULE

RNLI Navy Strength Gin 50ml
Lime juice 15ml
Ginger beer 50-100ml, to taste
Mint leaves to garnish

Build the liquids over ice in a tall glass and garnish with mint leaves – clap them between your hands first to release their oils.

www.conkerspirit.co.uk   01202 430384
Unit 3, 16a Inverleigh Road, Bournemouth, Dorset, BH6 5HA

TASTING NOTES

-

Forceful and flavoursome juniper
combines with tangy seville orange
and herbaceous, slightly sweeter
notes from marsh samphire and
juicy elderberries.

-

ABV 57%

CONKER COLD BREW COFFEE LIQUEUR

After a year of development, in 2017 Conker Spirit launched its Cold Brew Coffee Liqueur as a UK first - and it remains one of only a handful of drinks of its kind in the world.

Made without colourings, extracts or flavourings, this luscious tipple is a toothsome tribute to Grade 1 speciality Ethiopian and Brazilian coffee.

Cold Brew Coffee Liqueur is produced using Conker's British wheat vodka, finest speciality coffee and a touch of demerara sugar for a bold coffee flavour with cocoa hints and dramatic jammy fruitiness. It's a coffee liqueur, but not as you know it …

DISTILLERY
Conker Spirit

ESTABLISHED
2014

DRINK LAUNCHED
2017

LITRES PER YEAR
40,000

SISTER SPIRITS
RNLI Navy Strength Gin

Conker Port Barrel Gin

DISTILLERY TOURS
Available

SOLD ON SITE

PERFECT POURS

COLD BREW ESPRESSO MARTINI

Conker Cold Brew Coffee Liqueur 70ml
Water 30ml

Shake the Cold Brew Coffee Liqueur and water over ice for 20 seconds, before fine straining into a pre-chilled coupé glass.

CAFÉ SPRITZ

Pour classic indian tonic water into an ice-filled tumbler, then add 25ml of Cold Brew Coffee Liqueur. Garnish with a large wheel of fresh orange.

www.conkerspirit.co.uk   01202 430384

Unit 3, 16a Inverleigh Road, Bournemouth, Dorset, BH6 5HA

TASTING NOTES

-

Experience a satisfying depth of true, natural coffee
flavour with subtle hints of sweet black liquorice and
earthy cocoa, rich fruitiness and toffee.

-

ABV 25%

10 VIPER GIN

Founder of the Avalon Distillery Company Carl Hankey has a background in science and is also a chef with an MSc in nutrition, so when he decided to use his skills to produce an artisan gin it was odds-on that he would create a spirit of quality.

The result of much experimentation was this London dry gin, named after the rare snake which the Avalon team spotted when clearing land in Dorset on which to grow botanicals.

Avalon means 'island of apples' and, along with juniper and citrus, the gin has a subtle hint of crab apple. While it makes a great cocktail base, it's every bit as good in a G&T. Happily, there's no sting in the tail.

DISTILLERY
Avalon Distillery Company

ESTABLISHED
2018

DRINK LAUNCHED
2019

LITRES PER YEAR
5,000

SISTER SPIRITS
Viper Venom Gin

PERFECT POURS

GIN AND TONIC

Pour a measure of Viper into a highball glass filled with ice.

Top up with elderflower tonic and garnish with a slice or two of crisp Granny Smith apple and a single segment of star anise.

GARDEN OF EDEN

Viper Gin 25ml
Elderflower liqueur 10ml
Freshly squeezed lemon juice 5ml
Salt water 1 drop
Chilled Prosecco to top up
Lavender a sprig

Shake the first four ingredients together and strain into a flute glass. Add the Prosecco and garnish with a sprig of lavender.

www.viperspirit.co.uk   07539 433664

Unit 1, Blackhill Barn, Old Sherborne Road, Cerne Abbas, Dorset, DT2 7SJ

TASTING NOTES

-

A classic London dry style
but with gentle and slightly
sweet hints of apple and
vanilla. Streaks of fennel
and fresh citrus shine
through on the finish.

-

ABV 40%

11 BLACK COW VODKA

Black Cow is the only vodka to be made from grass-grazed-cow's milk, which results in an exceptionally smooth sip with a unique creamy character.

The Pure Milk Vodka™ is made at the Black Cow Distillery in the rolling west Dorset countryside.

Dairy farmer Jason Barber (who with Paul Archard started Black Cow in 2012) identified the potential of using the remains of the milk (the whey) once the cheesemaking process was finished.

He realised that whey could be utilised to make a milk beer and triple distilled to create vodka. And, inspired by tales of the Mongolian conquests, the journey to produce this outstandingly smooth vodka began.

DISTILLERY
Black Cow

ESTABLISHED
2012

DRINK LAUNCHED
2012

LITRES PER YEAR
170,000

SISTER SPIRITS
Black Cow + English Strawberries

DISTILLERY TOURS
Available

SOLD ON SITE

PERFECT POURS

DIRTY COW

Black Cow Vodka 60ml
Cocchi Dry Vermouth 50ml
Green olives 2, pitted and muddled (bruised) in a boston glass

Put vodka, vermouth and cubed ice to a jug or cocktail shaker and stir. Strain into a chilled martini glass and garnish with the olives.

BLACK COW ESPRESSO MARTINI

Black Cow Vodka 50ml
Lavazza Tierra fresh coffee 40ml, cooled
Maple syrup 15ml
Coffee beans 3, to garnish

Shake the liquids hard over ice, strain and serve in a martini glass. Garnish with the coffee beans.

www.blackcow.co.uk   01308 868844
Childhay Manor, Childhay, Beaminster, Dorset, DT8 3LQ

SPIRITS OF DISTINCTION

TASTING NOTES

-

A fresh and clean-tasting vodka
with admirable smoothness, and
roundness of texture. Its slightly
creamy, rich flavour is dry and
peppery on the finish.

-

ABV 40%

BLACK COW®
— VODKA —

* PURELY FROM MILK

THE GOLD TOP

40% ALC   WEST DORSET
ENGLAND   70 CL

12 E18HTEEN PASSIONFRUIT GIN LIQUEUR

Somerset gin maker Leigh Kearle founded E18hteen in 2016 and, after successfully launching his classic London dry gin, he expanded the distillery's repertoire to include a range of fascinating new flavours.

This Passionfruit Gin Liqueur is one of the offshoot creations and the exuberant, vivacious sip is currently the most popular addition to the inaugural juniper-led gin.

Like E18hteen's other drinks it's made from scratch, starting with a sugar-beet base spirit which delivers wonderful smoothness.

DISTILLERY
E18hteen Gin

ESTABLISHED
2016

DRINK LAUNCHED
2018

LITRES PER YEAR
100,000

SISTER SPIRITS
London Dry

Coconut Gin

PERFECT POURS

GIN LIQUEUR AND TONIC

Serve in a highball glass with ice, topped up with Luscombe Elderflower Tonic and a slice of fresh lime.

ON THE ROCKS

Chill hard and serve extra cold over ice with a wedge of lime. Garnish with a lime wheel.

www.18gin.co.uk   07789 222692

Hive Barn, North Petherton, Somerset, TA5 2BP

TASTING NOTES

-

A flavoured gin liqueur with
a fresh and natural aroma and
the vibrant, succulent, brightly
fruity flavour of passionfruit.
Delivers a lively tang with
balanced sweetness.

-

ABV 30%

13 NORTHMOOR GIN

After spending many years travelling the world in his role as an engineer – sampling a wide range of international gins along the way – John Smith decided to create his own spirit of distinction.

He founded Exmoor Distillery in 2017 and, after much experimentation, launched Northmoor Gin, which he named after the historic estate on Exmoor.

Distilled from ten carefully selected botanicals, it packs a punch at 44 per cent, with plenty of juniper flavour and complex underlying layers.

This is a fine gin designed to be served in a classic G&T or as the base for a quality cocktail.

DISTILLERY
Exmoor Distillery

ESTABLISHED
2017

DRINK LAUNCHED
2018

LITRES PER YEAR
8,000

SISTER SPIRITS
Navy Strength Gin

DISTILLERY TOURS
Available

SOLD ON SITE

PERFECT POURS

GIN AND TONIC

Pour a measure of gin into a glass with plenty of ice and add quality indian tonic to taste. Finish with a twist of lemon or lime.

CITRUS G&T

Replace the lemon or lime with a slice of blood orange or pink grapefruit.

www.exmoordistillery.co.uk   01398 323488
Unit 5, Barle Enterprise Centre, Dulverton, Somerset, TA22 9BF

TASTING NOTES

-

This is a bold gin with a compelling aroma and flavour, and bright juniper shining through. Expect notes of juicy citrus and spicy pepper and a rounded, lingering finish.

-

ABV 44%

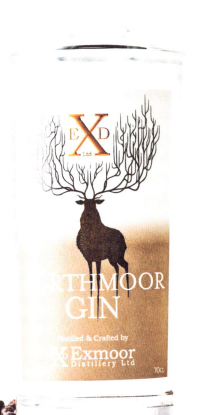

14 WICKED WOLF EXMOOR GIN

Pat Patel and Julie Heap experimented with gin recipes for two years before launching Wicked Wolf in 2015.

The pair eventually settled on 11 key botanicals - each individually distilled before being blended - as the key ingredients in this fresh and peppery gin.

Wicked Wolf is crafted in 100 litre batches in a copper alembic still at the Exmoor distillery, with the gin filtered at each stage of the process for maximum smoothness.

The contemporary spirit reflects Pat's passion for bold botanical flavours and reveals Asian influences: kaffir lime, cardamom, lemongrass and juicy hibiscus all feature in its bright yet elegant flavours.

Looking for a gin to match a fragrantly spiced dish? This could be the perfect pairing.

DISTILLERY
The Old Chapel Brendon

ESTABLISHED
2015

DRINK LAUNCHED
2015

LITRES PER YEAR
16,380

SISTER SPIRITS
Full Moon

Lorna Doone 1869

PERFECT POURS

GIN AND TONIC

Wicked Wolf 50ml
Premium tonic 200ml
Lime slice
Thyme a sprig

Pour the gin and tonic into a glass filled with ice. Garnish with lime and thyme.

ON THE ROCKS

Serve over a block of ice.

www.wickedwolfgin.com   01598 741357
The Old Chapel, Brendon, Devon, EX35 6PT

TASTING NOTES

-

Top notes of fresh citrus and
the distinct scent of kaffir lime
leaf are interwoven with more
traditional juniper and coriander.
Fresh and slightly peppery
on the finish.

-

ABV 42%

15 ATLANTIC SPIRIT #1 HIBISCUS

Distiller Quinton Davies and brewer Simon Lacey are both as obsessed with catching the perfect wave as they are with creating distinctive handcrafted gin, so it was clearly fate when they joined forces in 2017.

The pair use only premium botanicals sourced from north Devon's Atlantic coast and make their gin in copper pot stills using the traditional basket infusion technique.

#1 Hibiscus is distilled in 240-bottle batches with water sourced from nearby Tarka Springs. Dried hibiscus flowers provide a unique aroma and softness, while other botanicals - including liquorice root (for sweetness, not aniseed), citrus and spices - weave in additional layers of flavour.

DISTILLERY
Atlantic Spirit

ESTABLISHED
2017

DRINK LAUNCHED
2018

LITRES PER YEAR
6,000

SISTER SPIRITS
Lemon & Thyme

Thai Basil

SOLD ON SITE

PERFECT POURS

GIN AND TONIC

Serve #1 Hibiscus in a highball glass with a wedge of lime and plenty of ice.

AVIATION COCKTAIL

#1 Hibiscus 50ml
Fresh lemon juice 25ml
Crème de violette 25ml
Egg white 1

Dry-shake everything together in a cocktail shaker, then add ice and shake again. Double strain into a martini glass.

www.atlantic-spirit.co.uk   07402 626220

Abbotsham Road, Abbotsham, Devon, EX39 5AP

TASTING NOTES

-

Hibiscus flowers give a distinctive
aroma, a long juicy flavour and
softness to the gin. There's a pure
citrus lift from orange and lemon
zest, while cardamom adds a
subtle hint of spice on the finish.

-

ABV 42%

Atlantic Spirit

#1 HIBISCUS GIN

SMALL BATCH · HAND CRAFTED · ARTISAN
MADE WITH TARKA SPRINGS WATER

700ML ℮   42% VOL.

D&S DISTILLING CO. LTD   ABBOTSHAM · NORTH DEVON

PAPILLON GIN

Papillon Dartmoor Distillery's founders Claire and Adam Hyne grew up on the moor and are often out in the wilds, exploring on foot and by bike.

It was their experiences in this pristine natural environment that inspired their use of fresh gorse flowers, hawthorn and rowan berries, along with local Devon violets and camomile, in the creation of Papillon.

And the name? It's a reference to the Pearl-bordered Fritillary – an endangered Dartmoor butterfly. One per cent of sales from every bottle goes to the charity Butterfly Conservation.

DISTILLERY
Papillon Dartmoor Distillery

ESTABLISHED
2017

DRINK LAUNCHED
2018

LITRES PER YEAR
5,000

SISTER SPIRITS
The Admiral Navy Gin

PERFECT POURS

GIN AND TONIC

Papillon is best enjoyed sitting on a granite tor as the sun goes down.

Pour a double measure over ice, then add premium tonic and a small slice of lemon or lime.

ELDERFLOWER COLLINS

Papillon Gin 2 parts
Elderflower cordial 1 part
Fresh lemon juice 1 part
Sparkling water 5 parts

Mix the gin, cordial and juice in a glass filled with ice. Top up with sparkling water.

TASTING NOTES

-

Lemon and lime give fresh citrus;
cardamom and English coriander
create warm, spicy and peppery
notes; and gorse flowers, camomile
and Devon violets lend floral,
herbaceous hints.

-

ABV 42%

17 COPPER FROG GIN

Handmade in Exmouth, Copper Frog is a London dry gin created in a copper pot still (named 'Jenny') over an open flame.

Founder and distiller Simon Hughes prefers to use this naked-flame distillation process as he believes it brings out unique flavours and textures and lends the spirit a notable mouthfeel, although it requires a deft touch.

The gin is made in small batches with the 'heads' and 'tails' of the distillation discarded in favour of the more precious and flavourful 'hearts'.

Each bottle is hand filled, labelled and dip-waxed at the distillery - and each batch numbered and signed by every member of Simon's family, who are all involved in the business.

DISTILLERY
Copper Frog Distilling

ESTABLISHED
2017

DRINK LAUNCHED
2017

LITRES PER YEAR
8,000

SISTER SPIRITS
Copper Frog Black Edition Naval Strength

PERFECT POURS

GIN AND TONIC

Copper Frog Gin 50ml
Fever-Tree Light Tonic 100ml
Pink grapefruit to garnish

Serve in a glass with ice and garnish with pink grapefuit.

COPPER FROG'S FRENCH 75

Take a double measure of gin plus sugar syrup and grapefruit juice to taste. Shake over ice and strain into a cocktail glass. Top up with Champagne and garnish with a twist of pink grapefruit.

www.copperfrogdistilling.co.uk   01395 262636
Exmouth, Devon

TASTING NOTES

-

The fruity aroma of juicy
lime and pink grapefruit
is followed by a smooth,
rounded, fresh flavour and
texture. Finally, the warm
spice of pink peppercorn
comes through and lingers
on the palate.

-

ABV 42%

18 THUNDERFLOWER GIN

The tiny white thunderflowers that grow on Devon's thatched roofs are purported to ward off storms and witchcraft. Happily, only good spirits are at work in this gin named after them.

This small-batch London dry is made in one-shot distillation runs which extract the botanical flavours through vapour infusion. Two baskets are used: one large for the heavier botanicals, a smaller for more delicate ingredients.

This is a find for spirit lovers looking for a gin of classic character. Thunderflower features earthy and spicy notes from botanicals which include cassia bark, fresh sage, heather and cardamom.

DISTILLERY
Thunderflower

ESTABLISHED
2017

DRINK LAUNCHED
2018

LITRES PER YEAR
5,000

PERFECT POURS

GIN AND TONIC

Fill a rocks glass or stemless copa with ice and 40ml Thunderflower Gin, topped up with 100ml premium tonic. Garnish with a slice of fresh or dried citrus.

THUNDERFLOWER FRENCH 75

Thunderflower Gin 40ml
Fresh lemon juice 20ml
Simple sugar syrup 20ml
Chilled Champagne 60ml
Lemon zest long twisted spiral

Combine the gin, lemon juice and syrup in a cocktail shaker. Shake for 20 seconds. Strain into a flute glass and top up with Champagne. Garnish with the lemon twist. Alternatively, use Prosecco or English sparkling wine.

www.thunderflower.co.uk   01626 374055
Teignmouth, Devon

TASTING NOTES

-

An earthy, juniper-driven gin which
is dry and satisfyingly complex with
subtle spicy twists. Look out for the
notes of smoked black cardamom and
pink peppercorn on the lingering finish.

-

ABV 42%

19 SALCOMBE GIN 'ROSÉ SAINTE MARIE'

Inspired by the flavours and lifestyle of the south of France, 'Rosé Sainte Marie' is a fresh and smooth rosé gin, reminiscent of a balmy summer's evening by the Med.

Fragrant notes of fresh citrus peels and Provençal herbs add to the naturally sweet hint of red fruit. However, unlike many pink gins, there is no added sugar and the finish is purposefully dry.

The recipe was inspired by the fruits and herbs carried by the 19th century Salcombe fruit schooners, while the gin is named after the iconic Sainte Marie lighthouse at the port of Marseille.

DISTILLERY
Salcombe Distilling Co.

ESTABLISHED
2016

DRINK LAUNCHED
2019

LITRES PER YEAR
100,000

SISTER SPIRITS
Start Point

DISTILLERY TOURS
Available

SOLD ON SITE

PERFECT POURS

GIN AND TONIC

Serve in a large wine glass filled with ice, with premium indian tonic water at a ratio of 1:3 gin to tonic. Garnish with a strawberry or lemon peel twist.

SALCOMBE SPRITZ

'Rosé Sainte Marie' 25ml
Aperol 15ml
Fever-Tree Mediterranean Tonic to top up
Orange peel twist to garnish

Pour the gin and Aperol into a large wine glass with ice, then top up with tonic and garnish.

www.salcombegin.com   01548 288180
The Boathouse, 28-30 Island Street, Salcombe, Devon, TQ8 8DP

TASTING NOTES

-

A dry and soft, pale pink gin with
traditional juniper together with
strawberry and lemon verbena, fresh citrus
and a well-judged, subtle floral note from
lavender, rose petals and orange blossom.

-

ABV 41.4%

20 TREVETHAN CORNISH CRAFT GIN

This Cornish gin is a wonderful revival of a classic 1920s recipe crafted by Norman Trevethan at the Port Eliot estate.

Norman's grandson Robert Cuffe and head distiller John Hall breathed new life into Trevethan in 2015, refining the recipe while remaining true to the original by using handpicked Cornish hedgerow ingredients such as gorse flowers and elderflowers.

Exotic vanilla and cardamom accompany the local ingredients, but juniper is well to the fore in this complex but beautifully balanced London dry style.

The distillation has been refined in the modern age to create a fragrant and exceptionally smooth spirit.

DISTILLERY
Trevethan Distillery

ESTABLISHED
2015

DRINK LAUNCHED
2015

SISTER SPIRITS
Trevethan Chauffeur's Reserve Cornish Gin

Trevethan Grapefruit and Lychee Cornish Gin

SOLD ON SITE

PERFECT POURS

GIN AND TONIC

Serve over ice with a naturally light tonic, and finish with a large twist of fresh orange peel and a small sprig of rosemary.

TREVETHAN SOUTHSIDE

Trevethan Cornish Craft Gin 60ml
Fresh lime juice 30ml
Sugar syrup 15ml
Mint leaves 8

Add everything to a cocktail shaker filled with plenty of ice. Shake well, then fine strain into a chilled martini glass.

TASTING NOTES

-

An aromatic gin led by juniper and cut through by citrus, with floral notes and hints of vanilla and cardamom among the flavours. Soft, smooth and very lightly oily.

-

ABV 43%

21 ST PIRAN'S CORNISH RUM

This handcrafted Cornish rum is made by master distiller Dr John Walters using water from a well at the historic Treguddick Manor near Launceston.

The entire spirit is created from scratch: 100 per cent molasses is distilled three times in 200 litre copper pot alembic stills. The result is an exceptionally smooth rum with great depth of flavour.

St Piran's is named after the patron saint of Cornwall who brought fortune to the area with his discovery of tin mining ("white gold"), and its label features an illustration by Cornish artist Rosie Barlow.

A new distillery and visitor centre is due to open at the Manor in spring 2020.

DISTILLERY
English Spirit Distillery

ESTABLISHED
2011

DRINK LAUNCHED
2018

LITRES PER YEAR
250,000

SISTER SPIRITS
Old Salt Rum

English Spiced Rum

DISTILLERY TOURS
Available

SOLD ON SITE

PERFECT POURS

STRAIGHT UP

Sip and savour a white rum that's smooth enough to be drunk neat.

Serve over ice in a tumbler with a pinch of Cornish sea salt.

KERNOW LIBRE

St Piran's Cornish Rum 50ml
Coca-Cola 100ml
Lime wedge 1

Serve over ice cubes in a tumbler or highball glass. Stir and serve with a wedge of lime.

www.englishspirit.uk   01566 788310

Treguddick Manor, Treguddick, Launceston, Cornwall, PL15 7JN

TASTING NOTES

-

A satisfying, rich and gorgeously rounded soft rum. Although unflavoured, there are complex and subtle hints of sweet coconut, vanilla and banana in the finish.

-

ABV 42%

22 WRECKING COAST CLOTTED CREAM GIN

The Wrecking Coast Distillery founders Avian Sandercock, Craig Penn and Steve Wharton's ultimate aim when crafting their first spirit was to fashion a gin that would shine in a G&T, be bold as a cocktail base and, most importantly, stand on its own as that rarest of drinks - a sipping gin.

The use of Rodda's Cornish clotted cream in this gin makes it unique, and the distilling team cleverly retain the delicate flavours and texture of the ingredient by vacuum-distilling it separately.

Twelve robust botanicals - with juniper and coriander seed at the core - are precision distilled in high-tech apparatus to create a spicy base which envelopes the cream and delivers a dry gin loaded with flavour and complex textures.

DISTILLERY
The Wrecking Coast Distillery

ESTABLISHED
2015

DRINK LAUNCHED
2016

LITRES PER YEAR
20,000

SISTER SPIRITS
Cornerstone Gin

Honey Sloe Gin

PERFECT POURS

GIN AND TONIC

Allow sliced (or muddle fresh) strawberries to sit in the neat gin before adding ice and quality indian tonic.

ALTERNATIVE GARNISHES

Red berries work exceptionally well - strawberries or raspberries make the cream notes shine. Use blueberries with lemon zest as a worthy alternative.

www.thewreckingcoastdistillery.com

TASTING NOTES

-

A very smooth and rounded gin,
almost creamy in texture, though
not remotely sweet. Bright juniper
shines through while other
botanicals add a balance of warm
spice and freshness.

-

ABV 44%

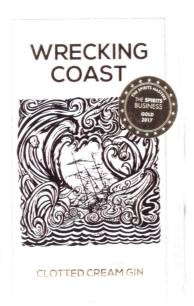

WRECKING
COAST

CLOTTED CREAM GIN

23 BLUE ANGEL ROCK GIN

The bright idea of creating the Cornish Rock Gin distillery came to its owners during a sunny walk on the beach at Rock with their dog Blue.

What started as a mere plan soon blossomed into an actual distillery in a beautiful wooded valley, featuring a still named Bonanza Boy (after a favourite racehorse).

The Blue Angel release is a very dry, naturally cobalt-hued gin made with blue gardenia flowers and grains of paradise spice which complement and enhance the other botanicals.

It's handmade using Cornish spring water, and not a single batch ever gets released without firm approval from neighbours across the river and local stockist The Little Gin Shack in Wadebridge.

DISTILLERY
Cornish Rock Gin

ESTABLISHED
2018

DRINK LAUNCHED
2018

LITRES PER YEAR
20,000

SISTER SPIRITS
Cornish Gold Rock Gin

Pink Cornish Rock Gin

DISTILLERY TOURS
Available

SOLD ON SITE

PERFECT POURS

GIN AND TONIC

Half fill a copa glass with ice, add a few blueberries, then pour in Fever-Tree Mediterranean Tonic and a double shot of Blue Angel Rock Gin.

DRY ROCK BLUETINI

Place a couple of blueberries in a martini glass, then half fill it with chilled dry white vermouth and top up with chilled Blue Angel Rock Gin.

www.rockgincornish.com   01208 851718

Penvose Cottage, St Tudy, Bodmin, Cornwall, PL30 3NP

TASTING NOTES

-

This gin is enticing
from the start with its
attractive natural blue
hue and floral nuances
on the scent. The flavour
is classically juniper-led
with a subtle spicy hit.

-

ABV 42%

PREMIUM CORNISH GIN
AUTHENTIC CORNISH

Blue Angel
CORNISH
ROCK GIN

MADE WITH UNIQUE
BOTANICALS AND
CORNISH SPRING WATER

70cl | 42% vol

BOTTLED BY HAND

BATCH NO: 2/034   SMALL BATCH

24 TARQUIN'S CORNISH DRY GIN

In 2013, self-taught master distiller Tarquin Leadbetter, then just 23, established the first new distillery in Cornwall for over a century.

After many trials, he created his popular gin which is now produced in 250 litre copper pot stills Tamara, Senara and Tressa, along with the newer 500 litre Ferrara.

It's a contemporary Cornish take on a London dry gin which uses violet flowers and orange zest among the botanicals.

Each of the distinctive bottles is wax sealed, labelled and signed by hand. Visitors on the distillery tours can have a go at waxing their own bottles as well as tasting a number of gins from Tarquin's Cornish collection.

DISTILLERY
Southwestern Distillery

ESTABLISHED
2013

DRINK LAUNCHED
2013

SISTER SPIRITS
The Seadog
Navy Gin

Tarquin's Rhubarb
& Raspberry Gin

DISTILLERY TOURS
Available

SOLD ON SITE

PERFECT POURS

TARQ AND TONIC

Tarquin's Cornish Dry Gin 50ml
Fever-Tree Mediterranean
Tonic 100ml
Pink grapefruit to garnish
Fresh thyme to garnish

Serve in a glass with plenty of ice. Garnish with pink grapefruit and fresh thyme.

CORNISH GARDEN SMASH

Tarquin's Cornish Dry Gin 50ml
Fresh lemon juice 20ml
Elderflower syrup 20ml
White vermouth 10ml
Pastis a dash
Cucumber 4cm slice, cubed
Herbs and edible flowers to garnish

Mix ingredients in a glass with ice and garnish with herbs and flowers.

www.tarquinsgin.com   01841 540121
Higher Trevibban Farm, Wadebridge, Cornwall, PL27 7SH

SPIRITS OF DISTINCTION

TASTING NOTES

-

Tarquin's Cornish Dry is a fragrant
gin with a floral note to the aromatics.
Classic juniper sweeps in on first taste
and there's fresh and clean citrus
on the finish.

-

ABV 42%

25 RATHLEE'S RUM

Stuart and Paola Leather (Rathlee is an anagram) may have roots in very different places - Cornwall and Colombia - but their shared passion for fine rum meant that creating a sip fusing Latin spirit and Cornish endeavour was a natural move.

After many tests and trial batches they perfected their house rum and the Rathlee Distilling Company was born. It also turned out to be the first fully-licenced rum distillery in the South West.

The rum is column distilled in Latin America before arriving on Cornish shores in charred white oak barrels, where it is carefully blended with pure Cornish water.

DISTILLERY
Rathlee Distilling Company

ESTABLISHED
2012

DRINK LAUNCHED
2017

LITRES PER YEAR
3,000

PERFECT POURS

CANCHÁNCHARA

Cornish honey 1 tbsp
Fresh lime juice 30ml
Rathlee's Rum 50ml
Water 30ml

Put the honey in a glass, then add the lime juice and rum. Mix with a barspoon until partially dissolved, then top up with a little water and ice.

RIGHTHANDER DAIQUIRI

Rathlee's Rum 50ml
Mango puree 50ml
Fresh lime juice 15ml
Sugar cane syrup 10ml (1:1 sugar to water)

Pour all the ingredients into a cocktail shaker with ice and shake for 20 seconds before fine straining into a coupé glass with a Cornish sea salt rim. Garnish with a lime wedge.

www.rathleedistilling.com   07775 845329
23 Cott Road, Lostwithiel, Cornwall, PL22 0EU

TASTING NOTES

-

A rum with satisfying and enticing
notes of tropical fruit, honey
and vanilla, with a warm pepper-
and-spice finish.

-

ABV 40%

26 ROSEMULLION SUMMER GIN

The Rosemullion Distillery was founded in the rural Cornish countryside in 2017 with the aim of using humble ingredients to create a perfect gin.

The team make the pure Cornish spirit from scratch at Rosemullion near Helford, distilling in a copper pot still and using Cornish rainwater. They control and assess all of the ingredients at every stage of the process to deliver on their objective.

This is a light gin with traditional juniper at the core and a kick of citrus and summery fruits including redcurrant, raspberry, blackberry and blackcurrant.

DISTILLERY
Rosemullion Distillery

ESTABLISHED
2017

DRINK LAUNCHED
2019

LITRES PER YEAR
10,000

SISTER SPIRITS
Rosemullion Dry Gin

Rosemullion Gold Rum

PERFECT POURS

GIN AND TONIC

Rosemullion Summer Gin 50ml
Fever-Tree Mediterranean
Tonic 150ml
Fresh raspberries 2-3

Serve in a highball or copa glass with ice.

SUMMER GIN MARTINI

Rosemullion Summer Gin 35ml
Briottet Rose Liqueur 25ml
Lillet Rosé Vermouth 15ml
Briottet Litchi Liqueur 7.5ml

Shake all of the ingredients with ice in a cocktail shaker, then fine strain into a martini glass.

www.rosemulliondistillery.com   01326 702202
25 Lemon Street, Truro, Cornwall, TR1 2LS

TASTING NOTES

-

Aromatic and juniper-centred
but with especially juicy and
succulent fruity flavours of citrus
and red berries. It finishes on a
fresh, vivacious note with just
a hint of mint.

-

ABV 40%

EXCEPTIONALLY AGREEABLE HAUNTS

Beautiful bars and lounges for libation

27 THE POTTED PIG

27 High Street, Cardiff, CF10 1PU

For adventures based around the classic pairing of pork and juniper, truffle out Cardiff's silhouetted porcine sign, then head down into the depths of this former bank vault.

'WELSH DISTILLERIES SPANNING SNOWDONIA TO THE GOWER PENINSULA'

The Potted Pig is a charming antidote to the chain bars across the city. It'll take several trips to work your way through its drinks list which features Welsh distilleries spanning Snowdonia to the Gower Peninsula.

Knowledgeable bartenders are also on hand to craft beautiful and bespoke cocktails, while the kitchen team deal in modern British fare with Welsh, French and New York grill influences.

ESTABLISHED
2011

ARTISAN SPIRITS
50

SEATS
70

FOOD
Served

www.thepottedpig.com   02920 224817

28 LAB 22

22 Caroline Street, Cardiff, CF10 1FG

Hidden in plain sight in the heart of Cardiff city centre, this first-floor cocktail den is worth seeking out on any trip to the Welsh capital.

'NO INGREDIENT IS OUT OF BOUNDS FOR THESE TECHNICIANS'

While its neighbours tout two-for-one deals and Sex on the Beach by the bucket, award winning Lab 22 concocts unique and inventive drinks experiences. The tenacious team of bartenders love to experiment with theatre, science and the senses, and curate an innovative collection of drinks to surprise and delight curious visitors.

No ingredient is out of bounds for these technicians, and they've even been known to refashion food waste from local restaurants into avant-garde ingredients. Regular events such as Monday Night Jazz provide further excuses to sample the eclectic bill of drinks.

ESTABLISHED
2012

ARTISAN SPIRITS
200

SEATS
80

EXCEPTIONALLY AGREEABLE HAUNTS

29 HER MAJESTY'S SECRET SERVICE

Whiteladies Gate, Whiteladies Road, Bristol, BS8 2PH

Tracking down this quintessentially British cocktail bar is not for the faint-hearted. Look for the white flag revealing a hidden entrance through an iconic red telephone box, then slide into the cosy drinking den, browse the assortment of artisan sips and get ready for a special spirits assignment.

ESTABLISHED
2015

ARTISAN SPIRITS
300

SEATS
60

'GET READY FOR A SPECIAL SPIRITS ASSIGNMENT'

Your codebook is a pocket-sized edition of *Winston's Illustrated Travel Guide to the British Isles* (a menu of quirky concoctions which takes imbibers on a tipsy trek through the UK).

Start with the Greenhouse Project – a dry and complex cocktail served in its own petite greenhouse. Then sip a Carless Vesper – a smooth, slick and shell-cased tipple inspired by the British Secret Intelligence Service.

www.hmssbristol.com   01179 733926

30 CRYING WOLF

37 Cotham Hill, Bristol, BS6 6JY

Home-crafted curations are given star billing at this chic Bristol bar - from the ingredients on its drinks list to the interior decor.

Firmly eschewing the bulk-buy mentality, all the shrubs, syrups and cordials (such as the vanilla and quinine syrup) are made from scratch, while juices are freshly pressed to order.

'SHRUBS, SYRUPS AND CORDIALS ARE MADE FROM SCRATCH'

The cocktail list changes seasonally, but past highlights include the Ocean of Storms (a punch made with rum, cognac, green tea, clarified milk, and pineapple and cardamom syrup), as well as a Rum Espresso which uses the Wolf's house-spiced spirit.

The team have worked closely with local artists and craftspeople to create the space, and the playlists are mastered by Bristol-based Massive Attack collaborator Stew Jackson.

ESTABLISHED
2018

ARTISAN SPIRITS
50

SEATS
75

FOOD
Served

HOUSE SPIRIT
Available

31 THE CLOCKWORK ROSE

16 St Stephen's Street, Bristol, BS1 1JR

While this cocktail bar was established in the 21st century, its quirky steampunk decor alludes to the 19th, so it's fitting that The Clockwork Rose has made its home on a historic street in Bristol's Old City.

The cocktail list is extensive and fascinating but, if you're stumped by what to choose, let us recommend an infused spirit such as cacao and ginger whisky, crafted in-house by the team.

'AN INFUSED SPIRIT CRAFTED IN-HOUSE BY THE TEAM'

Another unique must-try is the house Nautimore Victorian Gin, which is made with Bristol Dry and features soft citrus notes and a subtle smoky finish, care of lapsang souchong tea. For fin-de-siècle fabulousness, it has to to be a Montmartre Waterfall: Parisian absinthe and sugar with chilled mineral water slowly dripped over.

ESTABLISHED
2017

ARTISAN SPIRITS
10

SEATS
38

HOUSE SPIRIT
Available

EXCEPTIONALLY AGREEABLE HAUNTS

www.theclockworkrose.com   01179 276869

32 CHEWTON GLEN HOTEL & SPA

New Forest, Hampshire, BH25 6QS

If you're visiting this country house hotel on the Dorset and Hampshire border for its glamorous bar, its worth pushing the boat out and also booking a room for the night, as the drinks list is just one of the many delights to be discovered.

The 130-acre estate is also home to an award winning spa, nine-hole golf course, comp-standard croquet lawn, three restaurants and a cookery school (managed by James Martin) where you can distil your own gin under the expert tuition of Pothecary Gin founder Martin Jennings.

'DISTIL YOUR OWN GIN AT THE COOKERY SCHOOL'

Adventurous sippers will swoon over the regional gins and cocktails garnished with fresh pickings from the kitchen garden – try the petal-strewn Gypsy Pablo made with smoked vodka, truffle vermouth and desiccated serrano ham as a stonking aperitif.

ESTABLISHED
1966

ARTISAN SPIRITS
9

SEATS
180

FOOD
Served

EXCEPTIONALLY AGREEABLE HAUNTS

33 ACORN INN

28 Fore Street, Evershot, Dorchester, Dorset, DT2 0JW

If rural charm, an ancient setting and a 50-strong artisan spirit selection sound like a recipe for bliss, you'll want to schedule a trip to the Dorset countryside to visit this award winning 16th-century coaching inn.

'SIGNATURE COCKTAILS FEATURE GARNISHES PLUCKED FROM THE HERB GARDEN'

Open beams, crackling fireplaces and pups snoozing in the corner add to the idyllic country-pub vibe, but the real draw is the collection of craft spirits behind the bar. Sink into a comfy sofa while working your way through the extensive whisky and gin collection – bar supervisor Tomas is happy to advise.

Signature cocktails feature garnishes plucked straight from the inn's herb garden: try Dorset Conker Gin mixed with Grand Marnier and orange tonic, and studded with juniper berries, dried pear and star anise.

ESTABLISHED
2004

ARTISAN SPIRITS
50

SEATS
60

FOOD
Served

www.acorn-inn.co.uk   01935 83228

34 THE EASTBURY HOTEL

Long Street, Sherborne, Dorset, DT9 3BY

Behind the traditional entrance of this sophisticated Sherborne hotel lies a clubby bar with a classy cool all of its own.

With its leopard-print carpet, 1950s pin-ups and leather tub chairs, this is the kind of joint where Bing Crosby and Danny Kaye might have entertained a crowd in the Hollywood classic, *White Christmas*.

' THE KIND OF JOINT WHERE BING CROSBY AND DANNY KAYE MIGHT HAVE ENTERTAINED'

You'll find 15 artisan spirits on the list, with local Viper Gin being your best bet for a taste of the terroir. Take it as a classic G&T or opt for the house Gin Fizz which features Viper with elderflower cordial, soda, lemon and a sprig of mint.

Stay on for dinner: Matthew Street's two-AA rosette dishes are exceptional.

ESTABLISHED
1930

ARTISAN SPIRITS
15

SEATS
14

FOOD
Served

HOUSE SPIRIT
Coming soon

SALCOMBE GIN®

SALCOMBEGIN.COM

35 THE FIREHOUSE SOMERSET

Church Street, Curry Rivel, Somerset, TA10 0HE

This Somerset haven combines fine wines, local ales and handcrafted stone-baked pizzas with a craft spirit list to gladden the heart of any artisan drinks enthusiast.

Nestle into a plush armchair in the quirky bar and sip a G&T – the Salcombe Gin and elderflower tonic is a good call – or perch on one of the copper stools while the bartender crafts your bespoke cocktail.

'A CRAFT SPIRIT LIST TO GLADDEN THE HEART OF ANY ARTISAN DRINKS ENTHUSIAST'

The team are hot on making their own concoctions, too – check out the Firehouse Jumbleberry gin, Firehouse craft lager and the cocktail of the month.

A locally sourced menu offers plenty of delicious feasting options and, whatever the occasion or size of your party, there's an array of quirky areas and charming private dining rooms to suit.

ESTABLISHED
2016

ARTISAN SPIRITS
20

SEATS
120

FOOD
Served

HOUSE SPIRIT
Available

EXCEPTIONALLY AGREEABLE HAUNTS

36 THE BANK RESTAURANT & BAR

Middle Street, Taunton, Somerset, TA1 1SJ

For an exquisite craft spirit and gourmet sojourn in the heart of Taunton, you really need to bookmark 'The Bank under 'must-visit'.

'THE SIGNATURE COCKTAILS ARE BEST SIPPED ON THE SUN-SPLASHED ROOF TERRACE'

Inside the period building, original fittings and fixtures add charm to a smart yet comfortable restaurant which delivers both casual eats and more formal dining thrills.

Duck downstairs via the spiral staircase to the large bar area and pick a cosy nook in which to peruse a quality drinks menu of artisan spirits alongside craft beers and wines.

The team also mix a range of signature cocktails which, on warm evenings, are best sipped on the sun-splashed roof terrace.

ESTABLISHED
2015

ARTISAN SPIRITS
15

SEATS
72

FOOD
Served

www.thebanktaunton.co.uk   01823 257788

37 THE RISING SUN

Stout Lane, West Bagborough, Taunton, TA4 3EF

This thatched village inn may be steeped in tradition, yet the innovation going down behind the rustic oak bar ensures its drinks list is bang-up-to-date.

Whether infusing gins, ageing spirits, creating simple syrups or foraging for garnishes, the team at West Bagborough's much-loved pub are always musing over their next creative concoction.

'INFUSING GINS, AGEING SPIRITS AND FORAGING FOR GARNISHES'

Cocktails are devised with the seasons in mind, while the perfect gin and tonic is guided by the line-up of South West artisan spirits adorning the shelves.

Drinks are complemented by impressive dining-pub food made from regional and seasonal ingredients - true enthusiasts can even pair a Wicked Wolf and tonic with rainbow trout cured in the same spirit.

ESTABLISHED
2015

ARTISAN SPIRITS
40

SEATS
75

FOOD
Served

HOUSE SPIRIT
Available

www.therisingsunbagborough.co.uk   01823 432575

38 PETER MUNDY AT THE GINGER PEANUT

19 Fore Street, Bampton, Tiverton, Devon, EX16 9ND

Boutique distilleries are popping up in every rural corner of the region, but finding a stylish venue in the depths of the countryside where you can sip the results of their hard work is rare.

That's why The Ginger Peanut, with its smart take on out-of-town dining and imbibing, is a gem if you're exploring Exmoor National Park and the leafy lanes around Bampton.

'A SMART TAKE ON OUT- OF -TOWN DINING AND IMBIBING'

Mood lighting, wood panelling and plush plaid chairs create a delightful setting in which to delve into a 45-strong bar offering that deals in speciality whiskies, craft gins and rare spirits.

Chef Peter Mundy's locally sourced dishes are reason enough to visit, but it may be expedient to book one of the luxury bedrooms if you're taking advantage of Friday cocktail night or one of the regular gin events.

ESTABLISHED
2017

ARTISAN SPIRITS
45

SEATS
50

FOOD
Served

39 SQ BAR AND RESTAURANT

3 Exeter Road, Braunton, Devon, EX33 2JT

At the end of a busy day, it's hard to beat the pleasure of sitting on a rooftop terrace with a glass of something chilled to hand. And, with its views over bustling Braunton, SQ's rooftop space is the perfect spot for a chilled sundowner.

Choose your sip of choice from the stylish bar which harbours a 50-strong list of artisan spirits and offers a lavish cocktail collection. Then continue the indulgence by staying on for a supper of modern British classics.

'THE PERFECT SPOT FOR A CHILLED SUNDOWNER'

Lucy and Olly Seymour, the third generation of Braunton's restaurateur Squire family, have created a lively atmosphere at this popular post-beach stop-off and bolster the fun with gin festivals and events such as rum and reggae cocktail days.

ESTABLISHED
2014

ARTISAN SPIRITS
50

SEATS
120

FOOD
Served

40 CROCKETTS

2 Upper Paul Street, Exeter, Devon, EX4 3NB

You'll need to be in the know to locate Crocketts. Tucked away as it is on one of Exeter's cobbled side streets, the quirky little find is worth tracking down when you're in the Devon capital.

The Grade II-listed building that houses the bar is tiny, but with 130 spirits crammed onto the shelves this drinks haunt has one of the best collections anywhere. It even scooped Best Bar in the South West in the Food Reader Awards 2019.

Owner Lynsey Lowthian and bar manager Noah Cross are always adding new tipples to the endlessly shifting curation, but a good place to start is the house special, Copper Cameo, made with Crocketts' own gin.

'FOOD READER AWARDS' BEST BAR IN THE SOUTH WEST 2019'

Bespoke rum and gin tasting masterclasses and cocktail workshops are available for small groups.

ESTABLISHED
2017

ARTISAN SPIRITS
130

SEATS
52

HOUSE SPIRIT
Available

www.crockettsbar.co.uk 01392 332222

𝒜 RENDEZVOUS WINE BAR

38 Southernhay East, Exeter, Devon, EX1 1PE

Nestled in an Exeter sidestreet just a stone's throw from the Cathedral, this charming basement bar and restaurant is a favourite with discerning wine drinkers, spirit connoisseurs and bon viveurs.

An exciting and eclectic drinks list includes South West distilled gins, unusual spirits and more than 60 fine wines.

Sip your tipple inside surrounded by the rustic ambience of wooden beams, exposed brick and flagstone floors, or take it alfresco in one of the two hidden suntrap gardens.

'FOR DISCERNING WINE DRINKERS, SPIRIT CONNOISSEURS AND BON VIVEURS'

A daily-changing menu features locally sourced produce crafted into exceedingly good food, while the addition of occasional wine tastings and live music events make Rendezvous one to scribble in your little black book under 'city socialising'.

ESTABLISHED
2006

ARTISAN SPIRITS
30

SEATS
60

FOOD
Served

EXCEPTIONALLY AGREEABLE HAUNTS

www.rendezvouswinebar.co.uk   01392 270222

THE
WRECKING
COAST
DISTILLERY

CORNERSTONE
Rare Cornish
GIN
hand distilled with fresh pressed apple juice

MADE BY THE
WRECKING COAST
DISTILLERY

for Tom Brown

PROUD SPONSOR
OF THE
SOUTH WEST & SOUTH WALES
INDEPENDENT
GIN
& ARTISAN
SPIRITS
guide
EDITION 2

THEWRECKINGCOASTDISTILLERY.COM

42 DOCTOR INK'S CURIOSITIES

Customs House, 43 The Quay, Exeter, Devon, EX2 4AN

For an exquisite drinks experience imbued with wild creativity and a touch of the Victorian exotic, Doctor Ink's is an exceedingly charming find.

Imagine a drinking den with a hint of bordello and a dash of luxe chic, hidden within a Grade I-listed building, and you get the idea.

'TAKE THE DOC'S SEA-AIR CURE AT NEW SISTER BAR HALULU'

It's tiny and located just out of town on Exeter's quayside so you may have to hunt it out, but it's worth it for the innovative cocktails made from local and seasonal ingredients. Alternatively, take the Doc's sea-air cure at new sister bar Halulu on Teignmouth seafront.

ESTABLISHED
2016

ARTISAN SPIRITS
70

SEATS
25

FOOD
Served

HOUSE SPIRIT
Available

EXCEPTIONALLY AGREEABLE HAUNTS

www.doctorinks.com   01392 491695

43 THE HEADLAND HOTEL

Daddyhole Road, Torquay, Devon, TQ1 2EF

We've got a new fave T to pair with our G, and it's 'terrace'. At this elegant Torquay hotel, imbibing the house gin New Moon is best done on the sunny patio with its spectacular ocean backdrop.

On cooler days the modern Gallery Lounge, which opens onto the large clifftop terrace, is another great spot in which to work your way through the 20-strong artisan spirits collection while enjoying hazy horizons, balmy skies and evening sunsets.

'NEW MOON IS BEST IMBIBED ON THE SUNNY PATIO WITH OCEAN BACKDROP'

Botanical bevvies can also be paired with three, four or five courses in the Romanoff Restaurant (named after the Russian family who kept this clifftop villa as their holiday home) where dishes are fashioned around local farm produce.

ESTABLISHED
1859

ARTISAN SPIRITS
20

SEATS
192

FOOD
Served

HOUSE SPIRIT
Available

www.headlandtorquay.com 01803 295666

𝒜𝒜 PALACE HOTEL & SPA

Esplanade Road, Paignton, Devon, TQ4 6BJ

Perching proudly on Paignton's esplanade, the Palace Hotel makes a grand location for sipping a crisp gin and tonic.

The regal building is steeped in history. Head into the Washington Bar to sample a signature regional-gin cocktail while perusing snapshots of the hotel's former guise as The Palace for the Canadian Armed Forces in the second world war.

'A GRAND LOCATION FOR SIPPING A CRISP GIN AND TONIC'

Foodies will want to coincide their visit with a light lunch in the Colonial-style Sun Lounge or a six course (or à la carte) supper at The Paris Restaurant.

And, on warm days, there's no better place to unwind with a cool drink than on one of the outdoor sofas which offer sweeping coastal views.

ESTABLISHED
1925

ARTISAN SPIRITS
14

SEATS
95

FOOD
Served

www.palacepaignton.com   01803 555121

45 SALCOMBE HARBOUR HOTEL

Cliff Road, Salcombe, Devon, TQ8 8JH

It's not just a glistening waterfront that lures visitors to the yachty town of Salcombe; it also enjoys a reputation for artisan gin.

'FOLLOW COCKTAIL HOUR ADVENTURES WITH AN EXCELLENT SUPPER'

The attractive Crustacean Bar at chic Salcombe Harbour Hotel features a fabulous array of spirits as well as hosting gin tastings and daily cocktail masterclasses. Make a beeline for the signature Wicked Garden cocktail which features Tarquin's Gin, absinthe, elderflower liqueur and apple juice. If you're staying over, you'll also enjoy the decanters of complimentary gin and sherry in the bedrooms.

Follow cocktail hour adventures with an excellent supper at The Jetty restaurant, where you can indulge in fresh-from-the-water seafood, wines of distinction and panoramic views of the estuary.

ESTABLISHED
2013

ARTISAN SPIRITS
6

SEATS
85

FOOD
Served

⁴⁶ DARTMOOR INN

Moorside, Lydford, Okehampton, Devon, EX20 4AY

This recently refurbished inn on the edge of Dartmoor is well known for its foodie creds, but it also boasts a pleasing bar with a simple but well-curated spirit selection.

Start your supper visit with a Wicked Wolf gin from Exmoor or Black Cow Vodka from Dorset and you'll be on the right track.

'FOR A TRUE TASTE OF THE MOOR, LOCALS OPT FOR A TORS VODKA'

The team suggest pairing your pick with a Fever-Tree tonic or Luscombe mixer as the wide selection means there'll be something to complement any flavour profile. For a true taste of the moor, locals opt for a Tors Vodka.

There's also a variety of local beers and ciders, and the friendly welcome ensures every visitor leaves wishing this was their local. Charming and cosy guest bedrooms are an option if you really can't bear to go home.

ESTABLISHED
2019

ARTISAN SPIRITS
5

SEATS
80

FOOD
Served

www.dartmoorinn.com   01822 820221

DARTINGTON
CRYSTAL

PROUD SPONSOR OF THE

SOUTH WEST & SOUTH WALES
INDEPENDENT
GIN
& ARTISAN
SPIRITS
guide
2

DARTINGTON.CO.UK

47 THE FIG TREE @ 36

36 Admiralty Street, Plymouth, Devon, PL1 3RU

Showcasing the region's finest artisan produce is top priority at this neighbourhood restaurant – and this extends to a drinks list which features the likes of Salcombe Gin, Dead Man's Fingers Spiced Rum and Sandford Orchards juices.

'ADVENTUROUS SIPPERS CAN SET SAIL WITH A SALTY SEADOG'

Adventurous sippers can set sail with a Salty Seadog crafted from Cornish Todka (toffee vodka), Tia Maria, Cornish Orchards Ginger Beer and sea salt. Those looking for gems of the cocktail variety will be delighted to discover the Cornish Treasure Chest (Dead Man's Fingers Coconut Rum, Cornish Orchards Elderflower Presse, lime and mint).

Chef patron Ryan Marsland cooks up an equally creative menu with house specials which include Creedy Carver duck, slow-cooked Cornish pork belly and the local dayboats' latest catch.

ESTABLISHED
2019

ARTISAN SPIRITS
25

SEATS
40

FOOD
Served

48 BLUE PLATE RESTAURANT

Main Road, Downderry, Torpoint, Cornwall, PL11 3LD

Stepping into Blue Plate is like having all your senses walloped at once: a carefully curated collection of gins and spirits, stacks of freshly baked focaccia, house piccalilli, unusual wines, cheeses, books and an attractive bistro all vie for your attention.

'THE HOUSE ESPRESSO MARTINI FEATURES KALKAR CORNISH COFFEE RUM'

However, if it's artisan spirits you're in search of, you need venture no further than the deli out front where discerning locals and tourists spend evenings working through an interesting drinks list. Grab a seat at one of the butchers block tables and gorge on local seafood, pasture meats and sourdough pizza topped with seasonal produce.

Each of the artisan spirits is presented in a bespoke style, but for an uber local sip choose the house Espresso Martini made with Kalkar Cornish Coffee Rum.

ESTABLISHED
2010

ARTISAN SPIRITS
22

SEATS
70

FOOD
Served

www.blueplatecornwall.co.uk   01503 250308

49 OLD QUAY HOUSE HOTEL

28 Fore Street, Fowey, Cornwall, PL23 1AQ

A G&T (with a side order of stunning river views and a sea breeze) is the order of the day at the Old Quay House Hotel.

A sip of Salcombe Gin's Start Point introduces the palate to 13 botanicals sourced along the routes once frequented by ancient fruit schooners, and is perfect at a hotel that sits right on the Fowey estuary.

'GRAB A TABLE ON THE WATERSIDE TERRACE AND EXPLORE A 17-STRONG MENU OF ARTISAN SPIRITS'

Grab a table on the waterside terrace and explore a 17-strong menu of artisan spirits, as well as a cracking champagne selection. In addition, occasional pop-up events by Salcombe Gin provide an opportunity to sample new releases.

Those lingering for dinner in the stylish restaurant will get to pair drinks with the likes of renowned St Austell mussels and locally sourced lobster.

ESTABLISHED
2004

ARTISAN SPIRITS
17

SEATS
26

FOOD
Served

HOUSE SPIRIT
Available

www.theoldquayhouse.com   01726 833302

EXCEPTIONALLY AGREEABLE HAUNTS

50 THE BREAK BAR, BEACH HOUSE

Marine Drive, Widemouth Bay, Bude, Cornwall, EX23 0AW

Seafood, soul food, sunsets and signature cocktails ... there's nothing like a sundowner at The Break Bar.

Sunday garden parties at the laid-back Widemouth Bay venue include live beach jams, barbecues and the likes of Gin Sangria cocktails starring Tarquin's Cornish Dry Gin, Pinot Grigio, elderflower liqueur and ginger beer.

'SEAFOOD, SOUL FOOD AND SIGNATURE COCKTAILS'

With its terrace overlooking the ocean and private access to the sands at the bottom of the garden, this is a great spot for indulging in social events such as festive banquets on the beach and live lounges.

Cornish chef Alex Thompson's global cuisine scrumptiously fuses seafood and spices, and is complemented by the likes of Bajan-style Beachside Punch and Wild Beach Mint Mojitos.

ESTABLISHED
2016

ARTISAN SPIRITS
50

SEATS
80

FOOD
Served

www.beachhousewidemouth.co.uk 01288 361256

51 RUBY'S BAR

18 Broad Street, Padstow, Cornwall, PL28 8EA

Padstow's gastronomic reputation is no secret but this fabulous bar, tucked away from the bustling shopping streets, is one of the more hidden attractions in Rick and Jill Stein's family of food and drink favourites.

The private dining room will delight gourmets, but adventurous imbibers are sure to find enticing tipples (many of them Cornish) at the bar. One such sip is Tarquin's Rick Stein Gin - an exclusive gin made by Rick's son Charlie in collaboration with the Tarquin's team - which draws on botanicals of wild camomile and fennel to conjure up the Cornish coast.

'THE PRIVATE DINING ROOM WILL DELIGHT GOURMETS'

Discover a creative collection of house cocktails too: favourites include Espresso Martini, Rhubarb Bramble and the Mexican-inspired Ribs-e-Rita.

ESTABLISHED
2016

ARTISAN SPIRITS
30

SEATS
25

HOUSE SPIRIT
Available

www.rickstein.com/eat-with-us/rubys-bar   01841 532700

52 THE RISING SUN

Mitchell Hill, Truro, Cornwall, TR1 1ED

Gastro grub, craft spirits and barrels of bonhomie have turned The Rising Sun, a once derelict pub, into a thriving food and drink destination.

This Truro inn is the place to be on an August bank holiday weekend if you fancy alfresco food, acoustic sessions and copious amounts of glorious gin, as more than 100 craft and small-batch local, national and world gins are served from its rustic bar in the courtyard garden.

'GASTRO GRUB, CRAFT SPIRITS AND BARRELS OF BONHOMIE'

An elegant take on classic pub food is best anticipated with a pre-dinner Gin and Fizz cocktail or an Espresso Martini fashioned from Belvedere Vodka, Conker Cold Brew and Olfactory coffee.

Visit, too, for spirit tasting dinners and winter whisky tastings by the fire.

ESTABLISHED
2014

ARTISAN SPIRITS
30

SEATS
45

FOOD
Served

www.therisingsuntruro.co.uk   01872 240003

53 THE OLD GRAMMAR SCHOOL

19 St Mary's Street, Truro, Cornwall, TR1 2AF

The most important lesson to learn at this former Truro schoolhouse is which garnish and tonic best match each beautifully crafted local gin.

What was once Truro's grammar school has been turned into a playground for adults who visit to sample the stonking drinks list. Discover the work of classic distilleries alongside finds such as the nano-batch Westward Farm Gin from the Isles of Scilly.

'A PLAYGROUND FOR ADULTS WHO VISIT TO SAMPLE THE STONKING DRINKS LIST'

An impressive cocktail menu includes signature concoctions such as the Prosecco Flora: Caspyn Midsummer Dry Gin, elderflower liqueur and lemon, topped up with prosecco and garnished with edible flowers.

The indie restaurant and bar also makes a buzzing spot for relaxed casual dining and live music.

ESTABLISHED
2010

ARTISAN SPIRITS
70

SEATS
60

FOOD
Served

HOUSE SPIRIT
Available

www.theoldgrammarschool.com   01872 278559

54 THE ROSEVINE

Near Portscatho, Truro, Cornwall, TR2 5EW

There are many ways to enjoy the artisan spirits at this top-end, family-friendly hotel: sink a G&T while gazing upon glorious seascapes over Porthcurnick beach, sip a cocktail as you laze on a sun lounger or join family and friends for an aperitif on the manicured lawns.

The gorgeous Georgian house on the Roseland Peninsula offers the best of both worlds for parents with a penchant for the good things in life. There are lots of fun activities for kids while grown-ups are spoiled rotten with locally distilled spirits, carefully crafted cocktails and gin tasting evenings.

'A CLASSIC BRAMBLE MAKES THE PERFECT APERITIF'

A classic Bramble (served with a double shot of Tarquin's gin plus sugar syrup, fresh lemon and crème de mure) makes the perfect aperitif before feasting on a menu of fresh-from-the-waves-and-fields dishes.

ESTABLISHED
2001

ARTISAN SPIRITS
10

SEATS
30

FOOD
Served

www.rosevine.co.uk   01872 580206

55 DOLLY'S TEA ROOM

21 Church Street, Falmouth, Cornwall, TR11 3EG

For a taste of gin culture and old-school glamour in Falmouth, schedule a trip to Dolly's. Slip inside the green door and follow the strains of jazz upstairs to experience the trolley-load of tipples at this delightfully retro tearoom.

More than 320 artisan drinks, plus creative cocktails, are quirkily served in teapots and bone china teacups. The Holly Golightly is a house favourite and features Holly's Gin, Knightor Rose Vermouth, St Ives Pompelmocello Liqueur and Navas Cornish Tonic.

'COCKTAILS ARE QUIRKILY SERVED IN TEAPOTS AND BONE CHINA TEACUPS'

Make it a quintessentially British affair by pairing your G&T with a homemade scone. There are also the house pups Hebe (a pearl-adorned labrador) and Pearl (a springer spaniel) to coo over - both as delightful as the drinks offering.

ESTABLISHED
2011

ARTISAN SPIRITS
320

SEATS
40

FOOD
Served

www.dollysfalmouth.co.uk   01326 218400

Harbourside, Falmouth, Cornwall, TR11 2SR

Sea views, sumptuous spirits and stylish decor compete for your attention at this historic hotel overlooking Falmouth harbour.

A pair of chandeliers, fashioned out of glass whisky decanters, set the scene for stylish seaside sipping in the bar, park yourself on a plush sofa and work through an 80-strong spirits menu.

Sign up to get the deets on regular Gin and Rum Club events, which provide an opportunity to sample spirits from distinguished distilleries and the latest copper-pot pop-ups – as well as scrumptious food.

'SEA VIEWS, SUMPTUOUS SPIRITS AND STYLISH DECOR COMPETE'

Spirits can also be paired with the two -AA rosette dishes in the hotel's Water's Edge restaurant where the drinks list includes local vodkas, craft gins, artisan vermouths and award winning sake.

ESTABLISHED
1640

ARTISAN SPIRITS
80

SEATS
80

FOOD
Served

HOUSE SPIRIT
Available

www.greenbank-hotel.co.uk   01326 312440

57 PENVENTON PARK HOTEL

West End, Redruth, Cornwall, TR15 1TE

An eclectic mix of rich hues, ornate plasterwork and ancestral portraits add a dash of Georgian glamour to this family-owned hotel.

The copper bar makes an eye-catching centrepiece, the hand-beaten metal paying tribute to both the area's mining heritage and the craft of spirit distilling. Over 160 gins from around the world are stocked behind it, so pull up a stool or settle into a velvet chair in the lounge and peruse the list.

'SPIRIT TASTING BOARDS ADD THEATRE'

Spirit tasting boards add theatre to the Penventon Park experience and take the form of four measures and a mixer - or risk a game of roulette and let the wheel decide your fate.

On sunny days, a gin-themed afternoon tea party in the garden is rather special.

ESTABLISHED
1970

ARTISAN SPIRITS
160

SEATS
40

FOOD
Served

PURVEYORS OF IMPECCABLE SPIRITS

Stock your drinks cabinet with
unusual and specialist finds

Ginhaus Tasty Treats

- Cherry Frangipane   £1.75
- Chocolate Brownie (GF)   £2.95
- Really nice Strawberry Sponge   £2.50
- Coconut + Lemon Muffins   £2.95
- Pan Au Chocolate / Croissant   £1.60
- Iced Vanilla Latte   £2.80
- Rhubarb crumble w cream (GF)   £3.00
See deli for chilled cakes →

Gin of the day
Dictador
COLOMBIAN
aged in Oak barrels

58 FIRE & ICE

66 St James Street, Narberth, Pembrokeshire, SA67 7DB

It's worth scheduling extra time at this Pembrokeshire indie. Not only do visitors have the tricky task of choosing which beautifully designed bottle to add to their growing collection, there's also the difficult decision of which flavour of homemade gelato to devour on the way out.

ESTABLISHED
2011

ARTISAN SPIRITS
225

'OVER 225 SPIRITS LINE THE SHELVES'

Picking a winner is made even more difficult thanks to the abundant selection on offer: over 225 spirits line the shelves (175 of which are gins), flanked by a seasonal selection of Great Taste award winning ice creams and sorbets. In-store sampling and a knowledgeable team make things a little easier, and there are also regular tasting events at Narberth Museum. Alternatively, kill two birds with one cocktail and order a boozy sorbet such as a Dark and Stormy or a Mojito.

Fire & Ice specialises in Welsh spirits and for a taste of Pembrokeshire choose the Barti Dhu seaweed spiced rum.

PURVEYORS OF IMPECCABLE SPIRITS

www.fireandicewales.co.uk   01834 861995

59 GINHAUS DELI

1 Market Street, Llandeilo, Carmarthenshire, SA19 6AH

This gin lovers' haunt in rural West Wales is worth hitting the road to visit as it's so much more than simply an upmarket bottle shop.

A stonking 300 gins are currently stocked and, while it's a treasure trove of bottles to buy and take home, you'd be mad not to pull up a stool and experience its bountiful bar and incredible edibles.

'FIND WELSH GINS REPRESENTED ALONGSIDE LOCAL COALTOWN COFFEE'

The delicatessen, gin bar, coffee shop and open kitchen favours local produce, and Welsh gins sit alongside Coaltown Coffee (roasted nearby in the Amman Valley). Charcuterie, cheeses and antipasti also feature.

Swing by in the evening and, if you're lucky, you'll time your supper to coincide with one of the meet-the-producer or tasting events.

ESTABLISHED
2014

ARTISAN SPIRITS
300

60 WALLY'S LIQUOR CELLAR

10-14 Castle Arcade, Cardiff, CF10 1BU

Since 1981, Wally's Deli in Cardiff's Royal Arcade has been *the* place to stock up on artisan goodies and locally sourced treats. And, with the opening of its drinks-specialist sister venue in Castle Arcade in 2017, savvy day-trippers now arrive in the city armed with extra canvas tote bags.

Instead of charcuterie, cheese and preserves, visiting foodies leave the Liquor Cellar weighed down with local gins and rare whiskies from the 300-strong speciality spirits list. Welsh beers are also well represented.

'SIGN UP TO ONE OF THE REGULAR MASTERCLASSES OR TUTORED TASTINGS'

Luckily there's an extremely knowledgeable team on hand to guide visitors through the collection. Pop in on a Saturday for in-store sippings with local producers, or sign up to one of the regular masterclasses or tutored tasting events.

ESTABLISHED
2017

ARTISAN SPIRITS
300

www.wallysliquorcellar.co.uk   02920 233748

61 GREAT WESTERN WINE

Unit 3-4 Wells Road, Bath, BA2 3AP

For 36 years, Great Western Wine has sought out the very best wines, gins, artisan spirits and beers. And as a result of its award winning portfolio, the Bath bottle shop attracts not only oenophiles but gin and spirit connoisseurs too.

Find favourite gins like Curio, Trevethan and Salcombe alongside more unusual picks such as Copperhead's Black Batch Gin with elderberry and Ceylon tea.

'AN EMPORIUM-LIKE ATMOSPHERE'

The eclectic range of spirits creates a thrilling emporium-like atmosphere, but if you find choosing on the spot a little overwhelming you can also check out the range online and visit with your hit-list already in hand.

The team host regular wine tasting events and dinners to help customers take their wine and spirit experiences and knowledge to the next level.

ESTABLISHED
1983

ARTISAN SPIRITS
150

PURVEYORS OF IMPECCABLE SPIRITS

62 CORFE CASTLE VILLAGE STORES

25 East Street, Corfe Castle, Dorset, BH20 5EE

If you're visiting Corfe Castle, the beautiful and historic village at the heart of the Isle of Purbeck in Dorset, it's worth scheduling a visit to this something-for-everyone shop. As, alongside selling every kind of convenience item you could possibly imagine, owners Carole and Terry Birnie stock more than 330 gins.

While many tourists seek out the village to explore its ancient castle ruins, those in the know also make a pilgrimage to the Village Stores to peruse gins from local, national and overseas distilleries.

'TRY A TEENY TASTER BEFORE COMMITTING'

Sipping your way through hundreds of bottles to find a new favourite could prove an expensive mission. Happily, Carole and Terry invite customers to try a teeny taster before committing.

ESTABLISHED
2014

ARTISAN SPIRITS
330

PURVEYORS OF IMPECCABLE SPIRITS

63 MORRISH AND BANHAM
WINE MERCHANT & TASTING ROOM

1 Pope Street, Brewery Square, Dorchester, Dorset, DT1 1GW

This indie retailer is renowned for its acclaimed wine selection, but there's also an impressive compilation of spirits to be discovered.

Much of Morrish and Banham's 70-strong line-up of spirits hails from the local area. Bottles are always open so the team can guide you through samples but, if you have the time, let us recommend seating yourself in the tasting room for a G&T (or two).

In the summertime, the team welcome mobile distillery Still on the Move, which pops in to craft the bespoke Pope Street Gin. Keep an eye on social to find out when to swing by to bag one of the limited edition bottles.

'SEAT YOURSELF IN THE TASTING ROOM FOR A G&T (OR TWO)'

Drinks enthusiasts are also lured in by the gin tasting events, which are hosted by visiting distilleries and feature gins paired with charcuterie and cheese boards.

ESTABLISHED
2015

ARTISAN SPIRITS
70

61 TRADING POST FARM SHOP

Lopenhead, South Petherton, Somerset, TA13 5JH

Brimming with delectable local and organic produce - each nook and cranny reveals yet more delicious luxuries - this Aladdin's cave of gastronomic delights grants far more wishes than your typical farm shop.

Yet, despite its award winning success, the decadent bazaar remains true to its original ethos of selling regional organic cheeses, pies, veg and more in the heart of rural Somerset. Twenty years after opening, the treasure trove has continued to expand and now includes locally crafted ales and ciders, along with 30 of the region's finest artisan spirits.

'AN ALADDIN'S CAVE OF GASTRONOMIC DELIGHTS'

A gin sampling event takes place every month but there's no need to fret if you miss it - as you can also taste samples at the till.

Venture in to seek out the perfect accompaniment to your own fairytale dining experience.

ESTABLISHED
1989

ARTISAN SPIRITS
30

www.tradingpostfarmshop.co.uk   01460 241666

PURVEYORS OF IMPECCABLE SPIRITS

65 DARTS FARM

Topsham, near Exeter, Devon, EX3 0QH

From humble beginnings as a farm shop hut, Darts Farm has continually evolved over the past 40 years to become an incredible place to stock up on artisan food and drink in the South West.

While the award winning farm shop has long stocked a world-class collection of wines, beers, ciders and spirits, 2019 sees the launch of the Cider Innovation House - created in partnership with local producer Sandford Orchards - as well as the Darts Farm Drinks Cellar and Tasting Bar.

'THE DRINKS CELLAR SPECIALISTS HAVE ALMOST 100 YEARS' COMBINED EXPERIENCE'

The store showcases over 195 spirits, including a hefty selection of gins, so don't be shy about asking the knowledgeable team for advice: the Drinks Cellar specialists have almost 100 years' combined experience.

ESTABLISHED
1971

ARTISAN SPIRITS
195

www.dartsfarm.co.uk   01392 878200

66 THE TIPSY MERCHANT

13 High Street, Budleigh Salterton, Devon, EX9 6LD

With so many gins on the market, each with characteristics as unique as the palates of the people who sip them, it's great to know there are experts who can guide you through the process of finding your perfect tipple.

ESTABLISHED
2017

ARTISAN SPIRITS
150

'STAFF ARE HAPPY TO GUIDE VISITORS THROUGH THE COLLECTION OF 80 GINS'

This Budleigh Salterton drinks merchant may have started out specialising in new, old and historic wines but, as interest in gin and spirits has boomed, it has embraced local independent distilleries which favour artisanal methods of production.

Staff are happy to advise visitors navigating the curated collection of 80 gins – often bought direct from the distillers – which can be sampled in-store or at one of the tutored gin tasting evenings (with nibbles). And, once you've exhausted the gin list, there's a 70-strong spirits portfolio to investigate.

www.thetipsymerchant.co.uk   01395 443943

PURVEYORS OF IMPECCABLE SPIRITS

67 THE SHOPS AT DARTINGTON

Shinner's Bridge, Dartington, Devon, TQ9 6TQ

The Shops at Dartington (a rural shopping complex on the historic Dartington Estate) offers an exceptional curation of artisan products which encompasses everything from homewares to unique jewellery. Housed in former agricultural buildings, it's an ode to luxurious living.

The Food and Drink Shop is no exception, showcasing a range of gourmet products – 60 per cent of which are either grown, reared or made in the South West.

'THE ESTATE'S SIGNATURE GIN COMES IN THREE VARIETIES'

The estate's signature gin (named after Dorothy and Leonard Elmhirst who set up The Dartington Hall Trust charity) comes in three varieties and is distilled on the premises. It can also be imbibed at the on-site cafe and the White Hart Inn on the main estate.

Keep an eye out for gin-making classes at the distillery, and pick up a jar of Elmhirst Gin & Tonic Marmalade.

ESTABLISHED
1955

ARTISAN SPIRITS
12

68 BARBICAN BOTANICS GIN ROOM

38 New Street, Plymouth, Devon, PL1 2NA

Y ou may already be familiar with the online Little Gin Box subscription, but did you know that the team behind it also have a shop and gin room?

A 15th century merchant's house in Plymouth is the setting for this gin-porium, which lists an impressive collection of around 180 spirits – including the house Barbican Botanics Gin and Barbican Botanics Spiced Rum.

ESTABLISHED
2018

ARTISAN SPIRITS
180

'TO EXPERIENCE THE BREADTH OF FLAVOURS, THE GIN FLIGHT IS A GOOD CALL'

Try before you buy by working your way through the list at the in-house bar – to experience the breadth of flavours, the gin flight is a good call. In summer, the courtyard garden becomes a suntrap and provides the best seats in the house for sipping chilled G&Ts.

Visit too for meet-the-maker evenings and masterclasses where you can distil your own gin.

www.barbicanbotanics.com 01752 227091

69 TREVALLICK'S FARM SHOP & TEA ROOM

Caradon Farm, Pensilva, Liskeard, Cornwall, PL14 5PJ

Local Cornish produce is at the core of this indie retailer and cafe – and that includes its regional craft gin portfolio. The farm shop and tea room proudly stocks every Cornish gin it encounters and its spirits list currently stands at 65, although there are always new finds being announced on social media.

ESTABLISHED
2012

ARTISAN SPIRITS
65

'TURN A VISIT INTO AN OCCASION AND ORDER A GIN-THEMED AFTERNOON TEA'

Turn a visit into an occasion and order a gin-themed afternoon tea. Four craft Cornish gins, artfully paired with complementary tonics, accompany finger sandwiches, scones and cakes. And, should you discover a new fave, you can always buy a bottle to take home.

Sunny days call for a seat on one of the outdoor circular benches where you can enjoy unrivalled views of both Dartmoor and Exmoor. Be sure to pack a roomy shopper as there are plenty of arts and crafts, and foodie treats too.

70 THE LITTLE GIN SHACK

4 Polmorla Road, Wadebridge, Cornwall, PL27 7ND

After working for a major licensed-wholesaler for over a decade, Neil Roberts fulfilled his lifelong dream to open his own gin and spirit emporium in May 2018.

With the help of wife Lee, Neil has created a destination for gin buffs in Cornwall who want to fortify their spirit collection with new and interesting finds. His experience in the industry makes him a fount of knowledge – ask about any of the 160 bottles and he'll be able to give you the low-down on the drink and the distiller.

'A DESTINATION FOR GIN BUFFS'

In-store tasters come as standard and there are plans to introduce a dedicated bar in 2020. Look out for distiller evenings and, for a special occasion, gather the gang for a bespoke tasting event where three gins are matched with tapas-style small plates. There's also an online store with bottling, tasting and serving notes.

ESTABLISHED
2018

ARTISAN SPIRITS
160

www.thelittleginshack.co.uk   07740 639565

71 JOHNS WINES

Unit 2, Lemon Street Market, Truro, Cornwall, TR1 2QD

Situated among the throng of Truro's vibrant indies in Lemon Street Market, the fabulously stocked Liquor Cellar is a treasure trove of artisan spirits and the latest addition to Johns Wines. The fifth generation family business was established in St Ives in 1894 and is now run by brothers Tom and Sam Hanson.

With over 500 artisan spirits, 100 gins and a small selection of wines, the Cellar has a craft bottle to suit every palate. It's great fun exploring the gleaming array yourself or ask one of the spirit specialists to help you pick your perfect tipple (you can try before you buy).

'THE CELLAR HAS A CRAFT BOTTLE TO SUIT EVERY PALATE'

For more drinks inspiration, visit the flagship store in St Ives or pop into sister restaurant and bar Beer & Bird, where the team hold spirit tasting events throughout the year.

ESTABLISHED
2017

ARTISAN SPIRITS
500

PURVEYORS OF IMPECCABLE SPIRITS

www.johnswines.co.uk   01872 857020

72 CONSTANTINE STORES

30 Fore Street, Constantine, Falmouth, Cornwall, TR11 5AB

It may be off the beaten track, but those in the know journey to Constantine Stores for the largest selection of wines and spirits in the South West.

Once you've passed the general provisions at the front of the store, there's a vast drinks emporium to be discovered. Superior Cornish sips sit alongside rare whiskies and quality rums and gins on an inventory of 4,000 artisan picks.

'CORNISH SIPS SIT ALONGSIDE RARE WHISKIES AND QUALITY RUMS AND GINS'

The team's wealth of knowledge and experience is useful if you're stuck for choice and, after getting a sense of your taste, they'll help you find a new favourite to add to your collection.

Although some collectables are in-store only, you needn't worry if you're not a local as most of the impressive selection is available to order online for home delivery.

ESTABLISHED
1957

ARTISAN SPIRITS
4,000

www.drinkfinder.co.uk   01326 340226

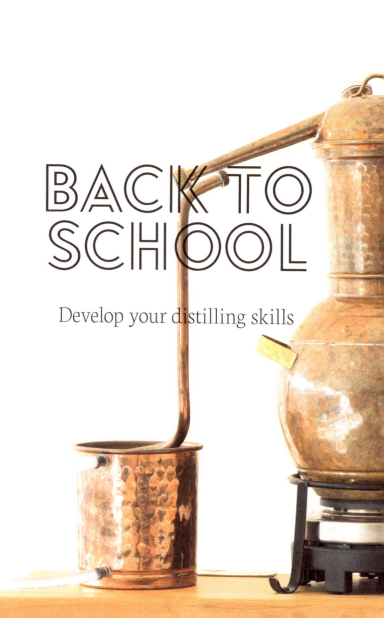

BACK TO SCHOOL

Develop your distilling skills

73 SALCOMBE GIN SCHOOL

The Boathouse, 28-30 Island Street, Salcombe, Devon, TQ8 8DP

For the true gin connoisseur, there's nothing quite like creating your own signature sip.

Amateur enthusiasts set sail for Salcombe Gin's waterside distillery, where they can concoct their own perfect blend of botanicals under the expert guidance of a master distiller.

Whether you know your palate is tuned to citrus or want to get experimental with florals and spices, the knowledgeable tutors take students through the distilling process and advise on which botanicals belong together.

'AMATEUR ENTHUSIASTS SET SAIL FOR SALCOMBE GIN'S WATERSIDE DISTILLERY'

The hands-on experience commences in style with a G&T and a tour of Salcombe's gleaming glass-panelled HQ, before aspiring spiritsmiths pull up a stool at the Gin School and get creative with their own mini copper pot still. The moment of glory is taking home a 70cl bottle of unique gin in a smart presentation box.

ESTABLISHED
2017

MAXIMUM GROUP
16

PRICES FROM
£110

www.salcombegin.com 01548 288180

More

EXCEPTIONALLY AGREEABLE HAUNTS

Additional finds for your little black book

BREWSTONE

33 Uplands Crescent, Uplands,
Swansea, SA2 0NP

www.brewstone.co.uk

THE DARK HORSE

7a Kingsmead Square, Bath, BA1 2AB

www.darkhorsebar.co.uk

THE DEAD CANARY

Barrack Lane, Cardiff, CF10 2FR

www.thedeadcanary.co.uk

DOOR 4

4 Montpellier Walk,
Cheltenham, GL50 1SD

www.door4montpellier.co.uk

GIN & JUICE

2-6 Castle Arcade, High Street,
Cardiff, CF10 1BU

www.ginandjuice.com

79

THE LIBERTINE

28 High Street, Cardiff, CF10 1PU

THE MILK THISTLE

Quay Head House, Colston Avenue,
Bristol, BS1 1EB

www.milkthistlebristol.com

NO.3

3 Fore Street, Topsham, Exeter, EX3 0HF

www.no3topsham.co.uk

THE RUMMER

All Saints Lane, Bristol, BS1 1JH

www.therummer.net

83

SPOKEN

43 The Strand, Exmouth, EX8 1AL

www.spokenexmouth.com

84

SUB 13

4 Edgar Buildings, George Street,
Bath, BA1 2EE

www.sub13.net

More

PURVEYORS OF IMPECCABLE SPIRITS

Additional finds for your little black book

85
THE BOTTLE SHOP
4 Pen y Lan Road, Roath, Cardiff, CF24 3PF

www.thebottleshops.co.uk

86
THE BOUTIQUE OF BOOZE
4 The Quay, Brixham, Devon, TQ5 8AW

the-boutique-of-booze.business.site

87
CHRISTOPHER PIPER WINES
1 Silver Street, Ottery St. Mary, Devon, EX11 1DB

www.christopherpiperwines.co.uk

88
THE CLIFTON CELLARS
22 The Mall, Bristol, BS8 4DS

www.cliftoncellars.co.uk

89
CORKS OF COTHAM
54 Cotham Hill, Bristol, BS6 6JX

www.corksofbristol.com

90
MUMBLES FINE WINES
524 Mumbles Road, Mumbles, Swansea, SA3 4DH

www.mumblesfinewines.co.uk

MEET OUR COMMITTEE

The *Independent Gin and Artisan Spirits Guide* committee have worked closely with the South West and South Wales drinks community in the creation of Edition 2

Susy Atkins

Consultant editor

Award winning drinks writer, presenter and author, Susy writes the weekly drinks column for the *Sunday Telegraph* and is drinks editor for *delicious.* magazine and *Food Magazine*. She also co-hosts *The Telegraph* Gin Experience each summer.

Susy enjoyed a 12-year stint as one of the regular wine experts on BBC1's flagship cookery show *Saturday Kitchen* and regularly appears with celebrity chefs presenting wines at food festivals and events in the UK and abroad. She is the author and/or editor of 11 books on drink and wine and has won several awards including a *Food & Travel Magazine* Readers' Award for Best Drinks Book.

Friday night tipple?

'A fine local gin with a light premium tonic (not too much) and two large ice cubes, garnished with a twisted slice of lime. Simple, clean, classic.'

Yohann Thuillier

Drinks consultant

Yohann has worked in some of the most prestigious hotels in the world, including Hôtel Plaza Athénée in Paris and The Dorchester in London.

He has polished his skills in various aspects of the trade in London, Paris, Bristol and Oxford before finally landing on the shores of Cornwall a few years ago. He took charge of the food and beverage operations at the Polurrian Bay Hotel and scooped F&B Manager of the Year in 2015 from *Boutique Hotelier* magazine.

He is currently based at The Greenbank Hotel in Falmouth and also oversees the bar and operations at sister hotel The Alverton in Truro.

Friday night tipple?

'If I'm out, a well-made classic cocktail like a Martini or Negroni.'

Rosanna Rothery

Food and drink writer

As features editor of *Food Magazine* (and a former restaurant critic on a South West newspaper), Rosanna has had gin-decent amounts of fun eating and drinking her way around the region for the past two decades.

Her love of a superb tipple and exquisite food began while working for London book and magazine publishers. However, as a West Country girl she's thrilled to be based in north Devon and writing for Salt's award winning Insider's Guide series (which includes *Trencherman's Guide* and the *Indy Coffee Guides*).

Friday night tipple?

'As Friday night is girls' night it is unapologetically a white-chocolate gin fizz cocktail.'

NOTES

Somewhere to keep a record of
interesting sips and venues

INDEX